Great Spuds

A Tribute to My Roots

Easy and Delicious Potatoes

Katherine Christie Wilson

Great Spuds: A Tribute to My Roots
KWIL Designs
5127 Glenwood Pointe Lane NE
Albuquerque, NM 87111
kwildesigns@gmail.com

Wilson, Katherine Christie
Great Spuds: A Tribute to My Roots
1. Authorship 2. Food Writing I. Title

Library of Congress Cataloging-in-Publication Data
is available from the publisher.

ISBN: 978-1-7923-2549-6

Cover Design and Photography by David Wilson
Layout and Text Design by Dickey Wilson
Drawings and Cover Illustration by Katherine Christie Wilson
Family Photos from Mary McGee

This cookbook is dedicated to my parents and grandparents,

Robert V. and Louise Holt McGee

Thurber E. Holt and Henrietta Bishop Holt

Thurber Holt in his potato field

Table of Contents

Thanks and Acknowledgements

Special thanks to:

David, for moral support, technical assistance, patience, and, most of all,
    for his appetite
Dickey, for editing, formatting and technical support
Mary, for family photos; Beatrice, for proofreading the narratives
Mary, Jerry, Roberto, Anna, Cheryl, Dawn, Judy and the many friends who
    have helped with this project by sharing and testing recipes
Puddy-Tat, for keyboarding assistance, pencil pushing, and oversight

The Farm, from the air, circa 1960

Part 1. Introduction

Great Spuds: A Tribute to My Roots

Potatoes have been getting a bad rap recently. People are decrying the obesity epidemic, and with good reason! Recent "food fights" in Congress have attempted to severely limit the portion size and number of servings of potatoes per week on school lunch menus. I do believe that potatoes themselves are not to blame for our national weight problems. While it is true that fried foods, including fried potatoes, contribute mightily to our expanding waistlines, the big culprit is the "fried" not the "potato." Let's learn to love this humble vegetable again, and let's learn to prepare it in healthy, tasty ways.

I grew up in a small town in Northern Maine where my grandparents were potato farmers. The whole culture of the community centered on the growing and harvesting of potatoes. Even as children we were involved. Many of us participated by cutting up seed potatoes for planting in the spring and pulling mustard and other weeds in the fields during the summer growing season. Come fall, everyone, (and I do mean everyone!), worked during the harvest. The harvest, known as "Diggin'," was so important that schools were closed for three weeks or more, so that everyone could help.

In late July, the fields of potatoes put out their sprinkling of white and pink blossoms. Acres upon acres of potato blossoms spread across the landscape. My small hometown of Fort Fairfield celebrated with the week-long "Maine Potato Blossom Festival," an annual tradition that continues today.

We ate potatoes every day, and sometimes we ate potatoes at more than one meal. We didn't know about "health foods," eating "local," or the dangers of a steady diet of fries and potato chips. French fries and potato chips were an occasional treat. We ate baked potatoes and mashed potatoes. We had home fries, which we called "hash," for breakfast. We had potato salad for lunch, and on special occasions we had baked, stuffed potatoes. When potatoes where not featured as themselves, they were usually included somewhere in other dishes, such as casseroles and stews.

2

It is my hope that you will want to include this healthy nutrient-packed vegetable in your diet, and that you will be inspired to try variations and new presentations.

Katherine

Katherine

The Story of the Potato

The potato (Solanum Tuberosum) is the fourth largest food crop in the world, behind rice, wheat and maize (corn).

Potatoes were first cultivated in South America, by the Incas, high in the mountains of the Andes, perhaps as long ago as 10,000 years. In the 16th century Spanish explorers, looking for silver and gold, found the potato. It was the principle food of the Incas of Peru. The Incas had developed a method of freeze-drying potatoes, which allows them to be stored for several years.

The potato was brought back to Europe by these early Spanish explorers in 1570. Potatoes were probably first introduced to Ireland in the 1600's by Basque fisherman traveling from northern Spain to the fishing grounds off Newfoundland. The potato had become a staple across northern Europe by 1750, and soon after became the dominant food in Eastern Europe and Russia. The popularity of the humble tuber continued to spread across Africa and Asia.

One legend gives Sir Francis Drake credit for introducing the potato to the British Isles and to Europe. In Offenbach, Germany, there was a monument to Drake that was destroyed during WWII. The inscription on the base of the statue said, "Disseminator of the potato in Europe, in the Year of Our Lord 1586. Millions of people who cultivate the earth bless his immortal memory." Other legends give credit to Sir Walter Raleigh, who may have planted potatoes on his estate in Ireland. Legends aside, many historians believe that the potato was the food source that eliminated famine in Europe and allowed a few European nations to become the dominant world powers between 1750 and 1950.

A French chemist named Antoine Parmentier published a paper on the nutritional value of potatoes in 1774. The potato yielded two to four times more calories per acre than wheat. It could supply essential nourishment for a nation that periodically dealt with famine. Potatoes were cheaper than rye bread, just as nutritious, and did not require a gristmill for grinding. Louis XVI championed the potato for French peasants. Marie Antoinette was said to have worn potato blossoms in her hair. In France, the name "Parmentier" is almost synonymous with "potato."

By the 1600's the potato had become a staple of the Irish diet. One acre planted in potatoes could feed a family of six for a year. Between 1780 and

4

1841 the population of Ireland doubled, thanks to this abundant and nutritious food source. In 1845, potato blight wiped out the entire crop. Due to dependence on a single variety, the Lumper, and lack of genetic diversity, the blight continued every year until 1852. The Irish peasants, who were totally dependent on their potato crop for sustenance, starved. Over a million people died and over two million emigrated, most of them to the US. In 1940 the population of Ireland was less than half what it had been in 1840.

The first potatoes in North America were planted in Derry, NH, in 1719, almost 150 years after their arrival in Europe. The popularity of the "spud," as it was called in England, grew rapidly. It was an ideal crop for the cool climate and acidic soils of New England. In addition to Maine, major crops are now grown in Idaho, Washington, Oregon and Colorado. It is the largest food crop grown in Canada. Potatoes are grown in every province, with major harvests in New Brunswick and Prince Edward Island.

Newer varieties of potatoes have greater resistance to blight. Botanist Luther Burbank developed new varieties of seed potatoes in the late 1800's, including one that bore his name. The Burbank potato is the botanical ancestor of the Idaho Russet.

The late 1800's also saw the appearance of the Colorado potato beetle (which, in fact, is not from Colorado), that led to the widespread use of pesticides. The first effective pesticide to be widely used was called Paris green. Over time the beetle became resistant to that pesticide. After WWII, farmers began to spray DDT on their crops but the pests and diseases kept returning. Varieties of newer chemicals are now used to control pests, blight and weeds, and to prohibit sprouting. This toxic treadmill has led to higher demand for organic produce.

Potato houses (barns) built partially underground or into a hillside, became common in the early 20th century. This allowed for better long-term storage and larger crops. Most potato houses were built alongside railroad sidings to facilitate transportation to markets.

There are over 4,000 varieties of potatoes grown in the world today. Some of the most popular are the starchy Russets, the waxy Red Bliss, and the all-purpose Yukon Gold and Katahdins. "New" potatoes, dug early in their growing season, are sweet and delicious. Small elongated potatoes called "Fingerlings" are similar to "new" potatoes, and can be found year round. Heirloom potatoes and blue potatoes are becoming more popular.

Potato House

Look for these symbols

Russets

Red, Waxy or All-Purpose

Small New or Fingerling

Helpful Hints

- One pound of potatoes will serve about three people.

- If a recipe calls for cooked potato, and you don't have a leftover begging to be used, your microwave can come to the rescue. Scrub the potato, prick several times with a fork, and place it on a plate. Microwave on high power for 4 to 6 minutes, turning it over halfway through. Using an oven mitt, pinch the potato to see if it is soft. Add more time in 30 second increments until the potato is cooked. More potatoes, or a very large potato, will take more time.

- Russets and long white potatoes are best for baking.

- If you have all of the ingredients prepped before you start, cooking will go much faster.

- Round red or white potatoes are best for potato salad.

- Potatoes will last several weeks if stored in a cool, dark place. The ideal temperature is 45 to 55 degrees. Keep them well ventilated in a mesh bag or the plastic bag with many holes that they came in.

- If you store your potatoes in the fridge, the starch may start to turn to sugar. You may notice a sweeter taste and they may darken a bit when cooked.

- Don't wash your potatoes until you are ready to eat them. Cut away any green spots and bruises, and cut out any sprouts.

Part 2: The Basics

"The County"

Basic Boiled Potatoes
Basic Mashed Potatoes
Basic Baked Potatoes
Toppers for Baked Potatoes
Roasted Potatoes
French Fried Potatoes

"The County"

Aroostook County is the largest county in not only Maine but all of New England. It also happens to be the largest county east of the Mississippi. If you fly over "The County" in a plane you will see that it is mostly wooded, with many lakes and rivers. You will see the land is cleared along the roads, and many of those cleared fields are growing potatoes.

When I was young and first saw a map of the United States, it seemed to me that Fort Fairfield—or Aroostook County at least—looked down on the rest of the world. All of the United States spread out under us to the south and then to the west. It was similar to the way my personal world spread out before my eyes, to the left and to the right, and way off into the distance. This was only a map thing, of course, because I knew that if I swiveled my head there was a lot of the world behind me. And if we looked to the east, there was Canada, just two miles away. Well, not all of Canada, but just beyond the Boundary Line Drive-In Theater was US and Canadian Customs. There was the Village of Perth-Andover, Victoria County, and New Brunswick. None of that was acknowledged on the map that hung in our classroom. As was common then, the map showed only the continental US, almost as though the much larger Canada did not exist. So we were all quite comfortable with the idea that we looked down on the rest of the world, all of the world that counted anyway. It was nice to feel so smug and superior.

Bangor, Maine, is the closest large city to Aroostook County. Large is relative, of course. Bangor had a population of 35,000 in the 1950's. It took almost four hours to travel the 175 miles, so we didn't get to the big city very often.

Basic Boiled Potatoes

This first recipe is basic boiled potatoes. They are the basis for many recipes, but also delicious on their own.

Helpful Hint: *Red or white round potatoes are the best choices for boiling.*

1. Scrub and peel the potatoes and cut them in uniform chunks.

2. Put them in a pot with enough water to cover them. Add 1 teaspoon of salt.

3. Bring to a boil over high heat. Partially cover the pot with its lid. Lower the heat just enough to maintain a low boil.

4. Boil until the potatoes are soft enough to be pierced with a fork. This will take about 20 minutes for 2" chunks, or about 15 minutes for 1" chunks or new potatoes.

5. Drain the potatoes in a colander and return them to the pot. Turn the burner to the lowest heat and shake the pot of potatoes over the heat for a few seconds, until the excess water has evaporated.

6. Serve with your choice of embellishments, or proceed with your recipe that calls for cooked potatoes.

Notes on New Potatoes: By late July farmers in The County are starting to dig very small, "new" potatoes. These flavorful delicacies need very little embellishment. I have recently found tiny potatoes in the supermarket. They are sometimes called "fingerlings" or "creamer" potatoes.

1. Wash the new potatoes gently to remove excess soil. Do not peel. Proceed as for Basic Boiled Potatoes. Check at 15 minutes and continue boiling until just barely tender.

2. Add butter and swirl to melt and coat the new potatoes. Salt to taste with salt and pepper, and serve with snipped parsley if desired.

Basic Mashed Potatoes

The ultimate comfort food! Round red, white or yellow potatoes make the best mashed potatoes. Russets work well too.

Helpful Hints: *I have seen potatoes mashed with a large fork or with two knives. The results will be chunkier, but still delicious! I have also seen mashed potatoes decimated in a food processor, whirled in a blender and pulverized by a hand mixer. This will produce a "smoothie" of potato glue. My advice is to use a potato masher and wrestle them to the ground with your forearm!*

4 servings

4 medium potatoes, about 1½ pounds, peeled and cut in chunks
1 teaspoon salt
¼ cup milk
1 tablespoon butter
Salt and black pepper, to taste

1. Put the potatoes in a pot with enough water to cover them. Add 1 teaspoon salt. Boil the potatoes until they can be easily pierced with a fork (about 20 minutes).

2. Drain the potatoes and return them to the pot. Shake the pot over low heat until the excess water has evaporated.

3. Add the milk and butter to the pot. Keep the burner on low for a few seconds more, until the butter has melted and the milk has warmed. Be careful not to boil the milk, which will make it curdle. (Alternately, warm the milk and butter together in the microwave.)

4. Remove the pot from the heat. Use a potato masher to mash to the consistency you like.

Yummy additions to mix and match: roasted garlic, minced parsley, horseradish, sour cream or plain (not vanilla!) yogurt. Reduce or eliminate the butter and milk if using sour cream or yogurt.

Note: If you prefer "smashed" potatoes, do not peel them. Use knives, forks, or a potato masher to smash the potatoes into chunky bits.

Basic Baked Potatoes

Please don't wrap the potatoes in aluminum foil! *This will produce a steamed potato not a baked potato. When it arrives at the table, the best baked potato will have a crisp and chewy skin, not wrinkled and soggy. And the potato flesh will be fluffy and light. Leave the foil concept to the restaurants where the potato will sit in a warm oven for many hours after it is baked, waiting to be served, and hoping not to become too dried out.*

Helpful Hint: Russets and long white potatoes are best for baking.

Preheat the oven to 400°.

1. Scrub the potatoes well and prick each one several times with a fork. This allows the steam to escape and keeps the potatoes from bursting in the oven.

2. Place them directly on the rack in your oven to bake.

3. Bake for 1 hour. To test for doneness, pierce with a knife to see if they are soft or, using a potholder, squeeze gently to see if they yield to pressure.

Helpful Hint #1: Potatoes really don't care how hot the oven is. If you are cooking something else in the oven at 350°, just plan to add about 10 minutes to the potato baking time.

Helpful Hint #2: Potatoes that are small (smaller than fist-size) will bake in less time. Very large potatoes will need more time.

Helpful Hint #3: If you are in a hurry for dinner you can "jump-start" your baked potatoes in the microwave while the oven is preheating. (Use full power for approximately 4 to 5 minutes for 4 potatoes, and adjust for fewer or more potatoes.) Then put the potatoes in the oven for 30 minutes. The skins will have a nice chewy texture if they are not completely cooked in the microwave, and if there is some actual baking time in the oven.

Toppers for Baked Potatoes

It is very easy to turn a baked potato into a satisfying and nutritious meal.

Helpful Hint: *Russets and long white potatoes work well for baking. Just make sure they are nice and fluffy once baked.*

Preheat the oven to 400°.

1. Bake as directed in Basic Baked Potatoes, page 11.

2. Using tongs to hold the hot potato, and a very sharp knife, cut a cross side to side and lengthwise on top of the potato. Squeeze gently to open the potato. Using a fork, gently fluff the potato inside. Put about 1 tablespoon of butter on the potato.

3. Now it is time to get creative!

Some tasty toppings and combinations:

> Grated cheddar cheese (always a good choice!)
> Sour cream with chopped red onion, or scallions, or chives
> Sautéed onions or caramelized onions
> Garlic butter
> Sautéed onions, mushrooms and green bell peppers
> Crisp bacon bits
> Diced ham
> Chopped, lightly steamed broccoli florets and grated cheddar
> Baked beans, grated cheese, sour cream and diced red onion or chives
> Chili, with beans or meat or both, and grated cheese
> Black beans and salsa
> Leftover roast beef and gravy

Roasted Potatoes

A healthy alternative to French fries!

Helpful Hint: *Russet, long white potatoes, and round yellow potatoes work well in this recipe.*

4 servings

4 medium white potatoes, about 1½ pounds
Non-stick cooking spray
2 tablespoons olive oil
4 cloves garlic, unpeeled (optional)
1 sprig rosemary (optional)
Salt and freshly ground pepper

Preheat the oven to 400°.

1. Choose a shallow roasting pan or casserole, large enough to hold all of the potato wedges in one layer.

2. Scrub each potato and cut into 6 or 8 uniform wedges.

3. Prepare the pan with non-stick cooking spray. Drizzle the olive oil over the potato wedges and toss in the pan until well coated with the olive oil. (Sprinkle with optional garlic and rosemary, if desired.) Salt and pepper generously.

4. Roast for 35 to 45 minutes, stirring and tossing at least twice. The potatoes are done when they start to look shriveled and brown in spots.

French Fried Potatoes

The first time I heard the term "fries" I was slightly offended. We always referred to them as "French" fries. That was many years ago, and I am now used to the popular term.

Helpful Hint*: If you have a deep fat fryer you are all set! You probably don't need any additional directions from me!*

Helpful Hint #2: *A mandolin is a useful tool for cutting uniform fries.*

6 servings

2 pounds russet potatoes, scrubbed and peeled (or not, your choice)
Oil for frying
Salt for serving
Malt vinegar or ketchup for serving

1. Trim off a slice of each potato so it will lie flat on the cutting board. Cut the potato into ¼" slices. Turn the stacks of slices and cut again into ¼" sticks.

2. Put the sticks in a large bowl of ice water and soak for at least 1 hour.

3. Pour 3" of oil in a large, deep pot. Heat the oil to 350°.

4. Drain the potato sticks and pat dry with paper towels.

5. Drop the potato sticks, a handful at a time, into the hot oil. Fry until limp and golden brown, about 6 to 8 minutes. Remove with a slotted spoon and drain on paper towels.

6. Repeat with remaining potato sticks.

7. Salt generously and serve immediately, with a sprinkle of malt vinegar or ketchup.

Part 3: Traditional and Favorites

The Real Maine Potato King

Baked Stuffed Potatoes
Variations on a Stuffed Potato

Growing Up On the Border

Potato Scallop
Another Potato Scallop
Hash Browned Potatoes
Home Fries

How a Boston Irish Boy Ended Up in The County

Crisscrossed Potatoes
Irish Nachos (Potato Skins Appetizers)
Scalloped Potatoes with Three Cheeses

The Real Maine Potato King

The Great Depression wasn't so bad, according to my mother. My grandfather, Thurber Eugene Holt, cleared the land using big draft horses, and planted potatoes. His potatoes were much in demand, and the best ones were sold to Bookbinders, a famous restaurant in Philadelphia. He also grew "certified seed potatoes," certified, that is, to be disease free.

During the Depression, "Grampy" put lots of people to work. He bought other farms and put the previous owners back to work for him. He built a large log "camp" on Portage Lake where he liked to entertain his fellow board members of the Bangor & Aroostook Railroad. I was only six years old when he died, but I remember him in a three-piece suit, driving around his potato fields in a big black Cadillac.

Family dinners on Sunday usually included a chicken, or sometimes a roast, and maybe a more dressed-up form of potatoes than the usual baked or mashed. Scalloped potatoes were a favorite, and Grampy loved baked stuffed potatoes!

Grampy

Baked Stuffed Potatoes

These delicious potatoes are often called "Twice-Baked Potatoes." They make wonderful dinner party fare. You can do all of the preparation in advance and heat them in the oven just before serving.

Helpful Hint: *If they are very large, each potato will yield 2 servings.*

6 servings

6 medium or 3 large potatoes
½ cup milk
2 tablespoons butter
Salt and black pepper
1 cup shredded cheddar cheese
Paprika

1. Prepare Baked Potatoes, page 13.

2. When the potatoes have cooled just enough to handle, cut a slice off the length of the potato. Slice the potatoes in half lengthwise if they are very large. Using a teaspoon, scoop out the potato flesh into a bowl, leaving potato shells about ¼" thick.

3. Mash the potato in the bowl along with the milk, butter, salt and pepper. Use a bit more milk if the mixture seems too dry. Blend in one-half of the shredded cheese.

4. Spoon the mashed potato mixture back into the shells. Sprinkle with the rest of the shredded cheese. Dust lightly with paprika.

5. Bake at 350° for 20 minutes or at 400° for 15 minutes, or until heated through and the cheese is melted. Add 5 minutes if the potatoes have been refrigerated.

Variations on a Stuffed Potato

Here are some ideas to spark your imagination!

Substitute other cheeses, such as Chevre, blue, or Gorgonzola for the grated Cheddar.

Use the following guidelines for 6 servings:

Mix with sautéed onions and mushrooms: Sauté 1 cup chopped onion and 6 chopped button mushrooms in 2 tablespoons butter. Mix some of the onion and mushrooms in with the mashed potato flesh. Spoon the mixture back into the shells and top with the rest of the onion and mushroom mixture. Bake at 350° for 20 minutes, until heated through.

Mix with broccoli: Steam and chop fine 1 stalk of broccoli. Mash potato flesh with 2 tablespoons butter, ¼ to ½ cup milk, salt and pepper. Mix in the chopped broccoli and ½ cup grated cheddar. Spoon mixture back into shells, and sprinkle with a little more grated cheddar. Bake at 350° for 20 minutes, until heated through.

Top with oysters: Omit cheese. Marinate 6 to 12 fresh raw oysters in ½ cup French dressing for 30 minutes. Mash potato flesh with 4 tablespoons butter, ¼ cup half-and-half, salt and pepper. Spoon mashed potato back into shells. Make impressions in each potato and press 1 or 2 drained oysters into each. Cover each potato with 2 tablespoons buttered bread crumbs. Bake at 350° for 20 minutes, until heated through and the crumbs are browned.

Mix with Roquefort cheese and green onion: Mash potato flesh with ½ to ¾ cups sour cream, salt and pepper. Mix in ¼ cup crumbled Roquefort and 4 finely chopped green onions. Spoon mashed potato back into shells, and sprinkle with paprika. Bake at 350° for 20 minutes, until heated through.

Growing Up On the Border

Fort Fairfield, where I grew up, is a small town in Northern Maine, nestled along the Aroostook River as it flows into Canada. The Village of Perth-Andover, New Brunswick, is just six miles away, and the boundary line is just two miles from the center of town.

The border in Northern Maine was not drawn until 1842, twenty-two years after Maine became a state. The people who live in the northern part of the state often refer to the other side of the border as "Over Home." And often you will hear our Canadian friends and relatives referred to as "Over-Homers."

There was a day when the border was much more "porous" than it is today. All the same, we did have to go through customs when we went back and forth, and there was a limit to the dollar amount of purchases you could bring back from Canada without paying duty. Smuggling was an art, practiced by many, and looked upon as a humorous and even competitive activity.

Smuggling worked both ways. We had Canadian friends who liked to shop on the US side of the border where many everyday items were cheaper or more readily available. Canadians usually drove over to shop without much gas in their tanks, and filled up on much cheaper gas before heading back. Our lawn was often littered with bags from Zayre, a popular discount department store back then, thrown out the window by Canadian shoppers headed home.

While many things were much cheaper on the US side, certain items were more available and of better quality on the Canadian side. We had a favorite store in Bristol, New Brunswick, for English bone china, Scottish woolen goods and Irish linens. In the fall we went on a shopping trip to Marich's in Bristol to round out the winter wardrobe with some fine tweeds and plaids.

Here's how it worked. With some of our potato picking earnings changed into Canadian currency, Mum, Mary and I would make a trip over to Marich's to shop for nice school clothes. We dressed for the occasion in a trench coat and a slip. We came back through US Customs wearing a couple of skirts (maybe a kilt! very popular in the 60's!), Liberty print blouses, a Scottish sweater or two or three, a wool scarf, and on top, the belted trench coat. At customs we would have to stop and roll down the car window so the agent could count people and ask us if we were all citizens. Then he would ask what we were bringing back from Canada. We would pat our tummies and say, "Just the big lunch we ate at York's!" Ha, ha.

One of my favorite smuggling stories involved my mother's dear friend, Norma. Norma was expecting a crowd for Christmas dinner, and she decided she needed a new tablecloth. Irish linen, of course. She donned her trench coat, drove over to Marich's, and bought a very beautiful, and very long, tablecloth. Norma was an ample woman already, but she wound the tablecloth round and round herself and belted herself into the trench coat. When she came back through US Customs she joked with the customs agent about having eaten way too much for lunch at York's.

Coming down the long hill from the border into Fort Fairfield, Norma's car hit a patch of icy road. She skidded off the road and hit a tree or a power pole, reports differ. Someone who witnessed this called the police about the accident. Norma's husband, the local undertaker, was also the ambulance driver. (Well, duh!) He heard the call on his police scanner, and hurried out to the scene. When he got to the scene of the accident, he found his wife. Norma was unharmed, thanks to being protected by yards and yards of Irish linen. So you see, smuggling has its rewards.

And what does this story have to do with potatoes, you might ask. Or recipes for anything? Norma, you see, was an excellent cook. Her culinary skills were legendary. I would love to share one of her recipes with you, but Norma never, ever, shared her recipes. If you were to comment on the deliciousness of her chocolate cake, and hint that you would love to have her recipe, she would say to you, "I will make this chocolate cake for you whenever you want!" And she would, too!

Potato Scallop

A traditional dish in The County.

Helpful Hints: *The secret to this dish is slicing the potatoes and onions very thin (with a mandoline, if you have one), and long, slow cooking. Too high a temperature causes curdling. Heating the milk in the microwave will hasten the cooking time a bit. Do not boil!*

6 to 8 servings

2 pounds (about 6 medium or 4 large) russets or all-purpose potatoes, peeled and sliced in ⅛" slices
1 large or 2 small onions (about 6 ounces), sliced in ⅛" slices
1 teaspoon salt
½ teaspoon freshly ground black pepper
4 tablespoons flour (or more)
3 tablespoons butter
2 cups milk (approximately)

Preheat the oven to 300°.

1. Lightly butter a 13" x 9" x 2" glass baking dish.

2. Layer one-third of the potato slices in prepared baking dish, overlapping slightly. Top with half of the onion slices. Sprinkle with salt and pepper and one-third of the flour. Dot with 1 tablespoon of the butter. Repeat, using the rest of the onion slices. Layer the last third of the potato slices, sprinkle with salt and pepper, the remaining flour and butter.

3. Pour milk evenly over the potatoes in the casserole until you can see it through the potatoes.

4. Cover the baking dish tightly with foil and bake for 1 hour. Uncover the dish and bake an additional 1 hour. Test with a knife to see if the potatoes are tender. If potatoes become too dry, add more hot milk during the cooking.

5. Remove from the oven. Let stand 15 minutes before serving.

Another Potato Scallop

Here is another take on a traditional favorite.

Helpful Hints: *The secret, once again, is slicing the potatoes very thin, and long slow cooking.*

8 servings

2 pounds (about 6 medium or 4 large) russet or all-purpose potatoes,
   peeled and sliced in ⅛" slices
4 tablespoons butter
1 medium onion, diced (about 1 cup)
2 cloves garlic, minced
4 tablespoons all-purpose flour
1 (14-ounce) can fat-free chicken broth
2 tablespoons mayonnaise
1 teaspoon salt
½ teaspoon freshly ground black pepper
Paprika

Preheat the oven to 325°.

1. Lightly butter a 13" x 9" x 2" glass baking dish.

2. Heat the butter in a large skillet. Sauté the onion and the garlic in the butter until soft.

3. Stir in the flour and cook, stirring, over low heat, for 1 minute. Gradually add the broth, stirring constantly. Add the mayonnaise, salt and pepper. Cook and stir for 2 minutes, until thickened. Add up to ½ cup of water if the sauce appears too thick.

4. Make three layers of the potato slices, spooning one-third of the sauce over each layer. Sprinkle with the paprika.

5. Cover the baking dish tightly with foil. Bake for 2 hours, or until tender. Test with a knife to see if the potatoes are tender.

6. Remove from the oven. Let stand 15 minutes before serving.

Hash Browned Potatoes

Better than the frozen stuff!

Helpful Hint: *Hash browned potatoes are grated, pan-fried potatoes.*

4 to 6 servings

4 medium white potatoes, grated
2 tablespoons butter
2 tablespoons canola oil
Salt and pepper

1. Heat the butter with the oil in a large frying pan until very hot but not smoking.

2. Add the grated potatoes, spreading to a depth of ¼".

3. Cook, covered, over medium heat until browned on the bottom.

4. Turn with a spatula and brown on the other side. Don't worry if you can't flip the potatoes all in one piece.

5. Add salt and pepper to taste and serve hot.

Home Fries

A Sunday morning treat, served with scrambled eggs and leftover beans! Home Fries were called "hash" when I was growing up.

Helpful Hint: *Plan ahead and bake or boil extra potatoes the day before.*

4 servings

4 medium all-purpose or Yukon gold potatoes, about 1½ pounds, cooked and cooled
3 tablespoons butter
1 tablespoon olive oil
½ medium onion, diced (about ½ cup)
Salt and freshly ground pepper

1. Peel the potatoes (or not, your choice) and cut into random-sized chunks, slices or cubes.

2. In a non-stick skillet melt the butter and olive oil together over medium heat. Add the onion and cook for about 1 minute, until just translucent.

3. Add the potato chunks. Season well with salt and pepper. Cook until heated through and turning golden brown, about 5 minutes, stirring occasionally.

4. Serve and enjoy!

Extras you might like to add: diced green bell peppers, bits of cooked meats, such as ham, corned beef or cooked bacon.

Mac and Louise

How a Boston Irish Boy Ended Up in The County

My father grew up south of Boston, in Brockton, Mass, where his father and his brothers worked in the shoe factory. I remember this important fact because, every now and then, one of the uncles would send Dad a new pair of golf shoes, which I imagined to have been smuggled off the line under a raincoat. Dad was the youngest boy. His mother died when he was quite young, and he was brought up and pampered by two older sisters and two older brothers. Part of the pampering was to make sure that he got a college education.

I believe there were priests at his Catholic high school who were involved in getting Dad a scholarship to play hockey at Colby. Although he was only 5'8" tall, he was scrappy and naturally athletic. During his career at Colby he was the captain of the football, hockey and baseball teams. While I was at Colby there were pictures of his teams from 1938 hanging in the corridor of the field house.

Dad, in the front row, center

We know that Dad did not spend four years in a row at Colby, but took time off to earn money so that he could return to college the next year. Good thing too, otherwise he might not have met Mum, the daughter of the Potato King, who was in the Colby class of 1940. Was it a pretty co-ed who lured him north to Aroostook County? Or was it an Irish thing, the lure of the spud?

Mum, Colby co-ed

29

Did the Boston Irish relatives serve traditional Irish dishes? Who knows? They certainly ate a lot of potatoes! I will give you a few of my favorites, and we can all just pretend that they were served in Boston, ah, actually...Brockton.

By the way, everyone who lives north of Boston refers to Massachusetts as "Mass." Just in case you were wondering.....

Crisscrossed Potatoes

A favorite with kids!!

Helpful Hint: *Russets are my favorites for this recipe. Large ones are usually available.*

6 servings

3 large potatoes
4 tablespoons butter, softened
Salt and pepper

Preheat oven to 400°

1. Scrub potatoes. Slice each potato in half lengthwise. Cut 1"-deep diagonal slashes in the cut side of the potatoes, and crisscross slashes in the other direction. Arrange in a baking dish.

2. Spread each potato half with about 2 teaspoons of the softened butter. Sprinkle generously with salt and pepper.

3. Bake at 400° for 45 to 50 minutes.

Irish Nachos (Potato Skins Appetizers)

A favorite for parties!!

Helpful Hint: *Small Russets work well for this recipe.*

16 appetizers

8 small baking potatoes, baked (page 13) and cooled
8 bacon strips, cooked and crumbled
3 tablespoons olive oil
½ teaspoon salt
¼ teaspoon garlic powder
¼ teaspoon paprika
⅛ teaspoon ground black pepper
2 tablespoons grated Parmesan cheese
1½ cups shredded cheddar cheese
½ cup sour cream
Chives or green onions, snipped

1. Preheat oven to 450°.

2. Cut potatoes in half lengthwise. Scoop out the pulp, leaving shells ¼" thick. (Save pulp for another use.)

3. Combine olive oil with salt, garlic powder, paprika and pepper. Brush over inside and outside of skins. Sprinkle insides with grated Parmesan cheese.

4. Place skins in a large baking pan and bake until crisp, about 12 to 15 minutes. Remove from the oven and sprinkle with shredded cheddar and reserved bacon bits.

5. Return to the oven and bake until cheddar has melted, about 2 minutes. Top with sour cream and sprinkle with snipped chives or green onions. Serve immediately.

Scalloped Potatoes with Three Cheeses

A favorite for holidays and potluck gatherings! Very rich and decadent!

Helpful Hints: *If you have a mandoline, this is the time to use it!*

Serving suggestion: *This is a wonderful addition to a ham or turkey dinner. It can be prepared several hours in advance and reheated in a 300° oven for about 20 minutes.*

6 to 8 servings

¾ cup (packed) grated sharp cheddar (about 4 ounces)
⅓ cup crumbled blue cheese (about 2 ounces)
¼ cup freshly grated Parmesan (about 1 ounce)
2 pounds russet potatoes, peeled and sliced in ⅛" slices (about 6 medium)
1 teaspoon salt
½ teaspoon freshly ground pepper
½ cup finely chopped onion
2 tablespoons flour
3 tablespoons butter
2 cups milk

Preheat the oven to 325°.

1. Lightly butter a 13" x 9" x 2" glass baking dish.

2. Mix the three cheeses in a small bowl.

3. Arrange half of potatoes in prepared baking dish, overlapping slightly. Sprinkle with half of the salt and pepper. Sprinkle the onion over the potatoes, followed by the flour. Dot with 2 tablespoons of the butter. Sprinkle with half of the cheese mixture. Top with the remaining potato slices and sprinkle with the rest of the salt and pepper. Dot with the remaining 1 tablespoon butter.

4. Bring milk to a simmer in a small saucepan (or warm to a simmer in the microwave). Pour the milk over the potatoes (milk will not cover the potatoes completely).

5. Cover the baking dish tightly with foil. Bake at 325° for 1 hour. Uncover the dish and sprinkle with the rest of the cheese. Bake an additional 50 minutes to 1 hour.

6. Remove from the oven. Let stand 15 minutes before serving.

Helpful Hint from Dawn: If you are a fan of blue cheese, consider increasing the amount!

Part 4: Summertime in Potato Land

The Country Club

Potato Salad
Potato Salad Variations
  Mediterranean
  German
  Greek

Diggin'

Lemon-Butter New Potatoes

The Camp

Potato and Pea Salad
Potato and String Bean Salad

Planting Potatoes

The Country Club

In 1929, during Prohibition, my grandfather and some of his contemporaries discovered the perfect solution to the pesky liquor problem. They built a country club and a golf course along the Aroostook River, with the club house and golf course on the Canadian side of the border, and the parking lot and pro shop on the American side. The Aroostook Valley Country Club is still very popular today, although there are still some pesky issues.

Access to the Aroostook Valley Country Club is only from the US side of the border, due to the bend in the river. For many years Canadian members and guests could avoid going through US Customs to get to the club, and avoid going through Canadian Customs on their way home, by coming across the border at the tiny Canadian border crossing at Four Falls. They had to drive directly to the club, about four miles south, and park in a specially designated part of the parking lot. No side trips to shop or fill up their cars with cheaper American gas!

Sadly our national security paranoia since 2001 has led to tightened border security, and the honor system for golfers is a thing of the past. Canadian golfers and guests must now travel an additional 21 miles to clear US Customs on their way over to the club, and Canadian Customs on the way home.

All of the staff who work at the clubhouse and the golf course must be Canadian citizens or have Canadian work visas. The opposite is true for those who work in the pro shop. Food from the kitchen must be purchased in Canada. And the booze, of course.

Mum and Dad were both avid golfers, and, as kids, we spent a lot of time at the Country Club. We played golf (not very well on my part), and caddied for a little spending money. If Mum was out on the course in the afternoon, we could count on a meal at the club. There was always potato salad.

Potato Salad

There are many, many variations on the potato salad theme. This recipe is basic and easy. Please experiment with the salad ingredients and dressing variations.

Helpful Hint*: Round red or white potatoes are best for potato salad.*

6 servings

4 to 5 medium red or white potatoes (about 1½ pounds)
The Dressing:
  ½ cup mayonnaise
  ½ cup plain yogurt
  1 tablespoon cider vinegar
  1 teaspoon Dijon mustard
  1 tablespoon sugar
  ½ teaspoon salt
  ¼ teaspoon black pepper
The Salad:
  1 stalk celery, sliced thin
  ¼ cup minced red onion
  ¼ cup green (or colored) bell pepper
Optional Garnishes:
  ¼ cup sliced green or ripe olives
  10 to 12 cherry tomatoes, halved
  Minced parsley

1. Scrub or peel the potatoes. Cut them in quarters and boil for 20 minutes, until soft. Drain the potatoes and allow them to cool.

2. Whisk the dressing ingredients together in a small bowl.

3. Slice or cube the cooled potatoes. Place in a large bowl. Add the celery, onion and bell pepper. Toss to combine.

4. Pour half of the dressing over the salad and toss. Continue to add dressing to the salad until you like the consistency.

5. Mound the salad on a serving platter and decorate with your choice of garnishes.

Mum tees off

Potato Salad Variations

Helpful Hint: Start with small, waxy potatoes.

6 servings

1½ pounds small to medium red or white potatoes

Scrub the potatoes, cut them in half or quarters, and boil for 12 to 15 minutes, until soft. Drain the potatoes and allow them to cool a bit.

Mediterranean Potato Salad

The Dressing:
   4 tablespoons olive oil
   1 shallot, finely chopped
   2 cloves garlic, minced
   2 tablespoons white wine vinegar
   1 tablespoon Dijon mustard
   ½ teaspoon salt
   ¼ teaspoon freshly ground black pepper
Add to the potatoes:
   1 tablespoon finely chopped chives
   1 tablespoon finely chopped tarragon (French), or ½ cup basil leaves,
      shredded (Italian)
   1 pint grape tomatoes (optional)
   1 cup sliced celery (optional)
2 cups baby salad greens, to serve

1. Make the dressing while the potatoes are cooking. Heat the olive oil in a small skillet. Add the shallots and garlic and cook, stirring, until they are softened, about 2 minutes. Scrape into a small bowl. Whisk in the rest of the dressing ingredients.

2. Cut the still-warm potatoes in smaller chunks into a medium bowl. Add some of the dressing and toss to combine. Add the herbs and toss again. Add

more dressing until you feel it is just right. Embellish with your choice of optional additions.

3. Arrange the salad greens on 4 to 6 plates. Mound the potato salad on the greens. Serve warm or chilled.

German Sour Cream Potato Salad

The Dressing:
1 cup sour cream (or ½ cup sour cream and ½ cup plain yogurt)
2 tablespoons cider vinegar
1 teaspoon sugar
¼ teaspoon dry mustard
1 teaspoon caraway seeds, crushed with the flat of a knife or with a
    mortar
½ teaspoon salt
¼ teaspoon freshly ground black pepper
Add to the salad:
½ cucumber, thinly sliced
2 scallions, minced
Optional additions:
4 slices bacon, cooked crisp and crumbled
hard boiled eggs, sliced

1.Whisk together the dressing ingredients.

2. Cut the cooled potatoes into smaller chunks in a medium bowl. Add some of the dressing and toss to combine. Add the cucumber and scallions and toss again. Add more dressing until you feel it is just right. Embellish with your choice of optional additions.

3. Serve chilled.

Greek Potato Salad

The Dressing:
   ⅓ cup olive oil
   1 clove garlic, minced
   2 tablespoons red wine vinegar
   1 tablespoon chopped fresh oregano (or 1 teaspoon dried, crumbled
      oregano)
   ½ teaspoon salt
   ¼ teaspoon freshly ground black pepper
Add to the salad:
   ⅓ cup Kalamata olives, chopped
   ½ cup crumbled feta cheese
   2 scallions, sliced
Optional additions:
   cherry or grape tomatoes, halved
   ½ cucumber, thinly sliced

1. Whisk together the dressing ingredients.

2. Cut the cooled potatoes into smaller chunks in a medium bowl. Add some
of the dressing and toss to combine. Add the olives, feta cheese and scallions
and toss again. Add more dressing until you feel it is just right. Embellish with
your choice of optional additions.

Potato Blossoms

POTATO PICKERS
WANTED

AROOSTOOK NEEDS YOU
-- FOR --
4-6 WEEKS WORK
GOOD WAGES

DO	DON'T
REGISTER AT ONCE With Your Nearest Public Employment Office -- Where All Information is Available About These Jobs.	Go to Aroostook County Until You Have Cleared With Your Nearest Public Employment Office. You Might Arrive Before You Are Needed!

Maine Employment Security Commission

Me. 114 (8-49)   MAINE UNEM ... 7 ...P. ...03
AUGUSTA, LOCAL OFFICE
331 WATER STREET
AUGUSTA, MAINE

Diggin'

Back then, and maybe even now, schools in The County started in mid-August, so that they could close down just a few weeks later for three weeks. Officially called the "Potato Harvest Recess," it was never referred to as anything but "Diggin'." The teachers probably referred to it as, "The time when the children forget everything we have taught them so far, and we have to start all over again."

During diggin' everyone, well darn near everyone, headed to the fields to pick potatoes. I was not allowed to pick until I was about nine. Many of my friends had been in the fields for a couple of years by then. Children were expected to earn money to buy their own school supplies and clothes, and save some to do their Christmas shopping.

We were up before dawn every morning, picked up in an old black panel truck with wooden benches, and delivered to the farm. The particular farm, to which we McGee kids were delivered, was owned by my great-aunt, who lived in the family homestead. She and my grandmother managed affairs on the farm, with the help of Alcide, the foreman. (In the early days of Women's Lib, I realized that the female role models in my family were strong, capable women, who sometimes told the men what to do.)

In addition to having our great-aunt, grandmother and mother lurking about all day, and delivering our lunch pails to the field at noon, we had the dubious distinction of having the cleanest clothes in the field. Mum washed and dried our mud-caked jeans and sweatshirts every night. We climbed back into the panel truck in the morning, feeling rather sheepish, and enduring some ridicule from the other pickers. It often took until mid-morning to get appropriately dirty again.

Okay, here's how it worked, for those of you who have never picked potatoes. Potatoes grow in rows, banked into low hills. When a field was ready to be harvested, the rows of potatoes were sprayed to stop their growth and kill the foliage. Then a rotobeater came along the rows and knocked down the tops of the plants. A tractor, pulling a digger, dug up two rows at a time, depositing the potatoes and any still-attached "tops" on the ground.

Pickers, who were arranged along the row, were each assigned a "section," the length of which should match the picker's ability and speed. (The length of each section was the cause of much squabbling and negotiating.) The picker shook off the tops and put her potatoes in a basket. When the basket was full, it was emptied into the picker's nearby barrel. A barrel holds three bushels, or 165 pounds. When the barrel was full, the picker slid one of her numbered tickets into the top hoop.

A flatbed potato truck, with a hoist, crawled along the field just a few harvested rows behind the pickers. As each barrel was hoisted onto the truck, the numbers were collected by the worker on the truck. In the evening, at the farmhouse, the numbered tickets were sorted and counted. When I was a kid, we earned 25 cents for each barrel picked. Many kids earned as much as $200 in a season, a small fortune in those days.

Nowadays the whole diggin' and pickin' process is done by a harvester, which dumps the potatoes into the back of a truck. I have stood by the side of the field and watched this, and I can assure you, it isn't nearly as much fun.

Lemon-Butter New Potatoes

If you feel like "gilding the lily," try this.

Helpful Hint: *You can melt the butter in a glass measuring cup in the microwave for a few seconds. Watch carefully!*

4 servings

1½ pounds new potatoes
⅓ cup butter
1 teaspoon grated lemon peel
3 tablespoons lemon juice
1 teaspoon salt
¼ teaspoon pepper
⅛ teaspoon ground nutmeg
2 tablespoons minced parsley

1. Wash the new potatoes gently to remove excess soil. Do not peel.

2. Put the new potatoes in a pot with enough water to cover them. Add 1 teaspoon of salt, if desired.

3. Bring to a boil over high heat. Partially cover the pot with its lid. Lower the heat just enough to maintain a low boil.

3. Boil until the potatoes are soft enough to be pierced with a fork. Check at about 15 minutes and continue boiling until just barely tender.

4. Drain the potatoes in a colander and return them to the pot. Turn the burner to the lowest heat and shake the pan of potatoes over the heat for a few seconds, until the excess water has evaporated.

5. Melt the butter and stir in the lemon peel, lemon juice, salt, pepper and ground nutmeg. Pour over potatoes and toss to coat.

6. Sprinkle with the minced parsley to serve.

The Camp

Sometime in the late 50's my parents arranged to buy the "camp" at Portage Lake from my grandmother. It seemed like a good place for a family of active kids to hang out in the summer, and I believe my parents enjoyed the social life around the lake as well.

Portage is a fairly big lake, about six miles long and a mile and a half across at its widest. Lots of room for paddling, sailing, swimming and water skiing. Mostly water skiing. Lots of water skiing.

The camp was a large log structure, built by my grandfather during the depression. Labor was cheap and plentiful then, and there were a lot of big logs left in the woods. The living room had an enormous stone fireplace and a soaring ceiling. The kitchen was also big, and the kitchen table could seat eight comfortably. A long screened porch faced the lake, and a second porch next to the kitchen had picnic tables for dining. Drinking water came from the hand pump in the dooryard*, washing water was pumped in from the lake.

Dooryard: A word that does not appear in the vocabulary of non-Mainers, apparently. It refers to the yard, just outside the door, usually the back door, the door everyone uses.

Mary and I shared the smaller bedroom, but we had access to the beds on the sleeping porch whenever we had friends visit. Bob and Charlie shared the loft, which had four beds and plenty of room for their friends. The most interesting feature in the loft was the bearskin rug, with its snarling mouth. The large master bedroom off the kitchen had room for two double beds and a crib. All counted up, there was sleeping space for 12 or more.

During my high school and college years we spent most of our summer days at the lake. We rarely missed a weekend, but as we grew older, we had summer jobs that kept us from full-time laziness, playing and partying.

Saturday evenings almost always featured a pot of baked beans. On Sunday mornings we would have hash with our eggs. This dish was more like "Home Fries" than "Hash Browns," but never mind that. We just called it "Hash." Leftover baked beans could put in another appearance on Sunday mornings too.

Mom liked to keep an eye on her kids, and the best way to do that was to make sure our friends felt welcome at our camp. I don't believe she ever ran out of hot dogs and hamburgers, and all those hungry teenagers and college kids knew it. The other thing she never ran out of was Sunday Beer. Back in those Dark Ages there were no Sunday liquor sales, and college kids, being what they are, rarely planned ahead very well. So by late in the day on Sunday, after much water skiing, the last few beers of the weekend could be found at our camp.

Along with all the hot dogs and hamburgers there would always be potato salad. And, quite often, the rest of the pot of beans.

Potato and Pea Salad

Fresh peas will turn this summer side dish into a gourmet delight. Buy them on the day you plan to use them, as the sugar in peas will convert to starch very quickly.

Helpful Hint: *You may substitute frozen baby peas, thawed, but not cooked.*

6 servings

The Salad:
  1 cup freshly shelled peas (about 1 to 1½ pounds in the pod)
  1½ pounds small red or Yukon gold potatoes, scrubbed and cut into ¼"
    slices
The Dressing:
  ¼ cup olive oil
  2 tablespoons white wine vinegar
  1 teaspoon Dijon mustard
  1 small clove garlic, minced
  ½ teaspoon salt
  ¼ teaspoon freshly ground pepper
Garnishes:
  ¼ cup fresh mint leaves, slivered
  ⅓ cup crumbled feta cheese

1. Simmer the peas in salted water until just barely tender, about 4 minutes. Drain and set aside to cool.

2. Boil the potatoes in a medium pot until just tender, 7 to 8 minutes. Drain and put in the refrigerator to cool while you make the dressing.

3. Whisk together the olive oil, vinegar, mustard, garlic, salt and pepper.

4. Pour the dressing over the potatoes in a serving bowl and mix gently.

5. Add the fresh (or recently thawed) peas, mint and feta. Toss gently. Serve chilled.

Potato and String Bean Salad

Fresh string beans from your garden are the best!

Helpful Hint: *Try mixing in some yellow wax beans if you can get them.*

6 servings

The Salad:
   1½ pounds small red or Yukon gold potatoes
   8 to 10 ounces fresh (green) string beans
The Dressing:
   ½ cup olive oil (divided)
   2 tablespoons red wine vinegar
   2 tablespoons fresh lemon juice
   1 small clove garlic, minced
   ½ teaspoon salt
   ¼ teaspoon freshly ground black pepper
   1 tablespoon, or more, snipped fresh oregano (or 1 teaspoon dried
      oregano)
   Pinch of red pepper flakes
Garnishes:
   Very thin slices of sweet onion
   Cherry tomatoes
   Snipped parsley

1. Boil the potatoes in a medium pot in salted water until not quite tender, 10 to 15 minutes, depending on size.

2. Add the string beans to the pot and return to a boil. Continue to cook about 4 minutes more. Drain potatoes and beans and set aside to cool while you make the dressing.

3. Whisk together ⅓ cup of the olive oil, vinegar, lemon juice, garlic, salt, pepper, oregano and pepper flakes.

continued...

4. Slice the still-warm potatoes into a large bowl. Toss with the remaining olive oil. Add the string beans, cutting very long beans in half.

5. Pour half of the dressing over the potatoes and beans. Mix gently and add more dressing, to taste.

6. Pile onto a pretty serving platter and sprinkle with more salt. (Use a fancy "finishing" salt, if you have it!) Decorate with the onion slices, cherry tomatoes and parsley. Serve chilled.

Parsley

Part 5: Mix-Em-Up

Cold Storage Room

Mashed Turnips and Potatoes
Cauliflower and Potato Gratin
Onion Potatoes
Roasted Root Vegetables
Ratatouille

Cold Storage Room

The cellar (basement) of our house had a cold storage room. There were rows of shelves filled with canned goods, jams and jellies, apples, tins of who knows what, and lots of empty tins, just waiting.

And there were large burlap bags of potatoes. There was always a bag of all-purpose potatoes, usually Katahdins, and a bag of baking potatoes, usually Russets. Sometimes there were Green Mountain potatoes, a delicious, fluffy baking potato. Green Mountains were not very resistant to blight, so they are practically nonexistent these days. In early August there would be a bag of "new" potatoes; small, round and delicious, with a short shelf life, even in the cold storage room.

In the late afternoon Mum would send one of us kids down to the cold storage room with instructions to pick out "six good-sized bakers" or a pot full of round potatoes to mash. It was a very rare supper that didn't include potatoes.

Mashed Turnips and Potatoes

You can use turnips or rutabagas for this dish. Many people love them. The rest will likely be converted by this recipe!

Helpful Hint: *The best kitchen tool for this preparation is a potato masher. I have also used a fork. The results will be a bit chunkier if you use a fork, but equally tasty.*

4 servings

1 pound turnip or rutabaga, peeled and cut in 1" chunks (about 2 cups
   when cut up)
2 medium (fist-size) potatoes, peeled and quartered
¼ cup orange juice
2 teaspoons brown sugar
1 tablespoon butter
Salt and pepper to taste

1. In a medium saucepan start boiling the turnip chunks while you peel and cut up the potatoes. Boil the turnips for 10 minutes.

2. Add the potatoes to the pot and boil for 20 minutes more, until the turnips and the potatoes can be easily pierced by a fork. Drain and return to the pot.

3. Add the orange juice, brown sugar, butter, salt and pepper. Mash well with a potato masher and serve while warm.

Cauliflower and Potato Gratin

Helpful Hint: The best kitchen tool for this preparation is a potato masher. You could also use an immersion blender at step 2.

Helpful Hint #2: You can make this ahead of time for your party. Cover and refrigerate the dish after step 5.

6 to 8 servings

4 medium (fist-size) potatoes, peeled and quartered
1 head cauliflower, florets and stems cut in 1½" pieces
2 cloves garlic, smashed
⅔ cup milk
2 tablespoons melted butter
½ teaspoon salt
Freshly ground black pepper
½ cup grated cheese (Cheddar, Fontina or Gruyere)
½ cup grated Parmesan cheese, divided

1. In a large pot start boiling the potato chunks while you cut up the cauliflower. Boil the potatoes for 10 minutes.

2. Add the cauliflower and garlic to the pot and boil for 10 to 15 minutes more, until the potatoes and cauliflower can be easily pierced by a fork.

Preheat the oven to 400°.

3. Drain the potato and cauliflower mixture and return to the pot. Mash well with a potato masher.

4. Warm the milk and 2 tablespoons of the butter in the microwave. Add most of the milk and butter to the potato and cauliflower mixture, until you like the consistency. Add more milk and butter if desired. Season with salt and pepper.

5. Stir in the grated cheese, including half the grated Parmesan. Turn the mixture into a greased 2 quart casserole dish. Sprinkle with the remaining grated Parmesan.

6. Bake at 400° for 15 minutes, until hot and bubbly. (If the dish has been refrigerated, add 10 to 15 minutes.) Broil for 1 to 2 minutes to brown the top, if desired.

Onion Potatoes

A great addition to a steak dinner!

Helpful Hint: *The foil-wrapped potatoes can be cooked on a barbecue grill or over a campfire for about 1½ hours.*

6 servings

6 medium potatoes
1 medium onion, sliced thin
4 tablespoons cold butter, more if needed
Salt and pepper

Preheat oven to 400°

1. Scrub potatoes. Cut through potatoes, almost to the bottom, making ½" slices.

2. Place a slice of onion and a thin slice of the cold butter between the potato slices. Sprinkle generously with salt and pepper.

3. Wrap each potato in foil and bake for 1 hour.

Roasted Root Vegetables

Roasting concentrates the flavors of vegetables, which makes this a good side dish to serve with a hearty entrée such as beef, lamb or pork.

Helpful Hint: *Choose a combination of root vegetables. Two pounds will provide 8 generous servings. Good choices include potatoes, sweet potatoes, carrots, onions, rutabagas, parsnips or yellow-top turnips. You may want to parboil or microwave the very hard vegetables (such as carrots or turnips) for 2 minutes to get them jumpstarted.*

8 servings

2 medium white potatoes
1 large sweet potato
2 carrots
1 medium onion
1 parsnip or turnip
¼ cup olive oil
5 cloves garlic, unpeeled
1 sprig fresh rosemary, or 1 teaspoon dried rosemary
Salt and freshly ground pepper

Preheat the oven to 400°.

1. Cut all the vegetables into bite-size pieces (about 1" square).

2. Pour the olive oil in a shallow roasting pan or casserole, large enough to hold all of the prepared vegetables in one layer. Toss the vegetables with the garlic and rosemary in the pan until everything is well coated with the olive oil. Salt and pepper generously.

3. Roast for 45 minutes, stirring and tossing at least twice. The vegetables are done when they start to look shriveled and brown in spots.

Ratatouille

Although this dish is of French origin, I have included it here because of the many other vegetables involved.

Helpful Hint: *Long, slow cooking over low heat is the key.*

8 or more servings

4 tablespoons olive oil
1 large onion, coarsely chopped
3 cloves garlic, minced
1 medium eggplant, peeled and cut into 1½" cubes
2 yellow summer squash, cut in ½" coins
2 small zucchini, quartered lengthwise and cut into 1" pieces
1 green bell pepper, cored, seeded, and cut in 1" pieces
1 red bell pepper, cored, seeded, and cut in 1" pieces
3 or 4 medium potatoes, cut in 1" cubes
Salt and freshly ground black pepper
½ cup finely chopped parsley
1 tablespoon finely chopped fresh basil (or 1 teaspoon dried basil)
3 or 4 fresh tomatoes, peeled and sliced
½ cup pitted green olives (pimiento-stuffed is OK)
Lemon wedges (for serving)

1. Using a large, heavy pot, sauté the onion and minced garlic in olive oil until soft.

2. Lower the heat and add, layering in this order, the eggplant, summer squash, zucchini, bell peppers and potatoes. Salt and pepper each layer generously. Add the parsley and basil.

3. Cover the pot with a tight-fitting lid. Cook over very low heat for 20 minutes.

4. Add the tomatoes and green olives. Check to see that there is some liquid in the bottom of the pot from the cooking vegetables. If not, add a small amount of boiling water. Continue to cook until potatoes are just tender, about 15 minutes more.

5. Serve hot or cold, with lemon wedges, if desired.

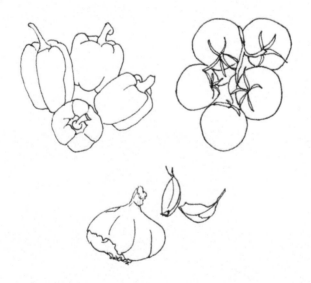

Part 6: Soups and Stews

Gram's Family

Clam Chowder
Corn Chowder
Fish Chowder
Cheesy Chowder
Vegetable Minestrone
Polly's Beef and Vegetable Soup

Henrietta's Recipes

Vichyssoise

Gram's Family

Henrietta (Gram) was born in 1899, which made her age easy to remember. On her birthday she would always turn one year older than the date. (Her great-great grandson, Charles Keohan, was born one-hundred years later, making his age easy to remember, too.) Gram passed away in 1989, just after her 90th birthday.

Henrietta's father, Max Bishop, was a potato farmer. Gram's siblings included Donald, Louise, Pauline and Mary Agnes. Many things were never, EVER talked about. Among them was the fact that Donald died of syphilis. The other was Louise Bishop's gender identity.

Louise never married. She lived all of her life in the big family farmhouse on the Caribou Road. She dressed in pants and flannel shirts and had her hair cut short, like a man's, by a barber. To say that Louise was a potato farmer would be fair, but the planting and harvesting were supervised by Alcide, the foreman. The family myth was that Louise fancied Alcide, and her heart was broken when he married another, which I think was nonsense. Alcide was very overweight and a good deal younger than Louise, so not someone I could imagine as her heartthrob, by any means. If the times had been different, Louise might have found a woman to love.

Louise Bishop, Potato Farmer

Gram was very fond of her sister, Pauline, who was just two years younger than she. Pauline died at age 11, of smallpox, I think. Gram gave me a small heart pendant engraved with a "P" that had belonged to Pauline. It appears to have teeth marks. Perhaps Pauline had a habit of biting her necklace.

Agnes, who was younger than Pauline, was remarkably independent. She was beautiful, and she married twice. Her first husband was a professional golfer named Cliff Roberts, who was the president of the Augusta National Golf Club in Georgia. Her second husband, the one I knew, was a Swedish arborist and inventor named Hjalmer Messing. Both of her husbands provided for her handsomely, and a good thing too! She had expensive tastes and unpredictable habits. She and Hjalmer lived in New York, on the East Side. But Agnes often came home to visit at the farm, to terrorize her sisters, and to shake things up a bit.

Henrietta was also a beauty. She was 16 and Thurber was several years older when they fell in love. Gram was sent off to Boston to LaSalle Junior College when she was 17, but she was very homesick and lovesick. She and Thurber were married in 1917, and my mother, Louise, was born in June, 1918.

Henrietta and Thurber

Clam Chowder

The best of Northern Maine (potatoes) and Coastal Maine (clams).

Helpful Hint: *For the best flavor, allow the chowder to sit for an hour, or overnight in the refrigerator. Reheat before serving.*

8 servings

2 to 3 pounds fresh clams
2 cups reserved clam broth
2 ounces salt pork, diced
1 medium onion, chopped (about 1 cup)
4 potatoes, diced (about 3 cups)
4 cups whole milk (or part half-and-half)
1 teaspoon salt
Freshly ground pepper to taste
4 tablespoons butter
4 tablespoons flour (optional, see note)

1. Rinse the clams and discard any that are broken or open. Put 1" of water in the bottom of a large soup kettle. Add the clams, cover and steam until the clams open, about 10 to 15 minutes. Remove the clams with a large slotted spoon. Strain the broth to remove any grit.

2. Shuck the clams and remove the black membrane. Chop the clams coarsely, saving any juice that you can.

3. Cook the diced salt pork in a large pot or Dutch oven over medium heat, stirring occasionally, until crisp. Transfer the crisp bits to a paper towel on a plate, using a slotted spoon. Discard all but 2 tablespoons of the drippings.

4. Add the onion to the reserved fat in the pot. Cook, stirring frequently, until softened, about 3 to 4 minutes.

5. Add 2 cups of the reserved clam broth (or the liquid from the cans of chopped clams), the diced potatoes and enough water or additional clam broth to cover the potatoes. Bring to a boil. Reduce the heat and simmer, stirring occasionally, until potatoes are soft, about 10 minutes.

6. Add the milk, clams, salt and pepper. Heat gently, but do not boil.

7. Swirl in the butter before serving. Garnish each serving with the reserved salt pork bits.

Note: If you prefer your chowder on the thicker side, you can make a roux with the butter and an equal amount of flour. Melt the butter over low heat in a small pot. Add the flour. Cook and stir for 1 minute. Stir some of the milk into the roux before adding it back into the chowder.

If you don't live near the coast, you can make this smaller, easier version. Start with step 3 and proceed with the above directions.

4 servings

2 ounces salt pork, diced
1 small onion, chopped (about ½ cup)
2 (8–ounce) cans minced clams, drained, clam juice reserved
2 potatoes, diced (about 2 cups)
⅔ cup water, or as needed
2 cups whole milk (or part half-and-half)
1 teaspoon salt
Freshly ground pepper to taste
2 tablespoons butter
2 tablespoons flour

Corn Chowder

The best of Northern Maine.

Helpful Hint: *If corn on the cob is not available you can substitute one (15-ounce) can cream style corn and one (15-ounce) can yellow or white corn in step 4.*

6 to 8 servings

5 to 6 ears fresh corn on the cob, shucked and steamed for 5 minutes
2 to 3 ounces salt pork, diced
1 medium onion, chopped (about 1 cup)
1 cup water
3 all-purpose potatoes, diced (about 2 cups)
2 cups whole milk, divided
1 cup half-and-half
1 teaspoon salt
Freshly ground pepper to taste
2 tablespoons butter
2 tablespoons flour (optional, see note)

1. Cut the corn kernels from the cobs, when cool, reserving any juice you can. You should have about 4 cups of corn.

2. Cook the salt pork in a large pot or Dutch oven over medium heat, stirring occasionally, until crisp. Transfer to a plate, using a slotted spoon. Discard all but 2 tablespoons of the drippings.

2. Add the onion to the reserved fat in the pot. Cook, stirring frequently, until softened, about 3 to 4 minutes.

3. Add the water and the diced potatoes and bring to a boil. Reduce the heat and simmer, stirring occasionally, until potatoes are soft, about 10 minutes.

4. Add 1 cup of the milk, half-and-half, corn, reserved corn juice, (or the cans of corn and creamed corn), salt and pepper. Heat gently, but do not boil.

5. Melt the butter over low heat in a small pot. Add the flour. Cook and stir for 1 minute. Gradually stir in the reserved cup of milk. When the roux starts to thicken, stir it into the chowder. Continue stirring until the chowder has thickened a bit.

6. Garnish each serving with the reserved salt pork bits.

Fish Chowder

A traditional chowder with old-fashioned flavor!

Helpful Hint: *Haddock, cod or cusk will work well in this recipe. Salmon will give the chowder a nice pink color!*

4 servings

2 ounces salt pork, diced
1 small onion, chopped (about ½ cup)
⅔ cup water
2 potatoes, diced (about 2 cups)
1 pound fish fillets
1 teaspoon salt
Freshly ground pepper to taste
2 cups whole milk
1 cup half-and-half or evaporated milk
Common crackers, to serve

1. Cook the salt pork in a large pot or Dutch oven over medium heat, stirring occasionally, until crisp. Transfer to a plate, using a slotted spoon. Discard all but 2 tablespoons of the drippings.

2. Add the onion to the reserved fat in the pot. Cook, stirring frequently, until softened, about 3 to 4 minutes.

3. Add the water and the diced potatoes and bring to a boil. Reduce the heat and simmer, stirring occasionally, until potatoes are almost soft, about 5 minutes.

4. Place the fish fillets on top of the potatoes and sprinkle with the salt and pepper. Cook over low heat until the potatoes are tender and the fish just barely flakes. If you stir, be gentle. The fish should be in fairly large pieces, not mushy.

5. Pour in the milk and half-and-half or evaporated milk. Heat gently, but do not boil.

6. Garnish each serving with the reserved salt pork bits. Pass common crackers to break up and sprinkle on top.

Note: *Common crackers are, well, common in Maine. If you can't find any, saltines will do. Be aware of the extra saltiness of the saltines.*

Cheesy Chowder

Great on a cold winter's night!

Helpful Hint: *You can omit the bacon in step 1 and use 2 tablespoons of butter in place of the bacon drippings.*

4 to 6 servings

3 to 4 strips bacon, diced
1 medium onion, chopped (about 1 cup)
2 cloves garlic, minced
2 cups low-salt chicken broth
1 carrot, sliced thin
1 rib celery, sliced thin
3 medium russet potatoes (about 1½ pounds), diced in ½" cubes
¼ cup flour
2 cups whole milk, cold
4 ounces sharp cheddar cheese, shredded (more to serve, if desired)
Freshly ground pepper to taste
Snipped chives (optional)

1. Cook the bacon in a large pot or Dutch oven over medium heat, stirring occasionally, until crisp. Transfer to a plate, using a slotted spoon. Discard all but 2 tablespoons of the drippings.

2. Add the onion and garlic to the reserved fat in the pot. Cook, stirring frequently, until onion is softened, about 3 minutes.

3. Add the chicken broth, carrot, celery and diced potato. Add water, if needed, to just cover the vegetables. Bring to a boil. Reduce the heat and simmer, stirring occasionally, until potatoes are soft, about 15 minutes.

4. Whisk the flour and cold milk together in a small bowl until perfectly smooth. Stir into the hot soup gradually, stirring continuously, until thickened.

5. Add the shredded cheddar. Heat gently to melt the cheese. Season with pepper.

6. Garnish each serving with the reserved bacon bits, snipped chives, and more shredded cheddar, if desired.

Vegetable Minestrone

Healthy, low-fat and vegetarian!!

Serving Suggestion: *Make it a meal with Italian bread and a simple green salad.*

8 or more servings

¼ cup extra virgin olive oil
1 medium onion, chopped (about 1 cup)
3 cloves garlic, minced
1 large stalk celery, sliced
1 large carrot, roughly chopped
1 leek, white and pale green parts only, washed and chopped
1 teaspoon dried oregano
1 teaspoon dried basil
1 teaspoon salt (or more, to taste)
½ teaspoon freshly ground black pepper
2 russet potatoes, peeled and diced (about 2 cups)
½ medium red or green bell pepper, seeded and chopped
1 medium zucchini, trimmed and chopped (about 1½ cups)
1 (15-ounce) can cannellini beans, drained and rinsed
1 (15-ounce) can diced tomatoes, with their juices
1 cup tomato juice
1 (15-ounce) can vegetable broth
2 cups water, or more if needed
¼ cup dry white wine
½ cup frozen peas
1 cup loosely packed chopped fresh spinach
½ cup loosely packed flat-leaf parsley, coarsely chopped

Optional garnishes:
    grated parmesan cheese
    fresh basil leaves

1. Heat the olive oil in a very large pot or Dutch oven. Add the onions, garlic, celery, carrot and leek. Cook, stirring frequently, until the vegetables are soft, about 5 minutes.

2. Add the oregano, basil, salt and pepper. Stir well to blend and cook for 1 minute more.

3. Add the potatoes, bell pepper, zucchini, beans, diced tomatoes with their juice, tomato juice, and vegetable broth. Add water, if needed, to cover the vegetables. Bring to a boil, reduce heat, cover, and simmer until the vegetables are fully cooked, about 20 minutes.

4. Stir in the white wine, peas, spinach and parsley. Bring to a boil again, reduce heat and simmer, covered, 5 minutes more.

5. Serve with optional garnishes.

Helpful Hint: *You may cool, cover and refrigerate the soup for up to 3 days, or freeze it for up to 2 months.*

Polly's Beef and Vegetable Soup

This recipe has been passed down for four generations! My mother-in-law, Polly, discovered this delicious soup when she combined her recipe for braised beef with a recipe for vegetable soup.

Serving Suggestion: *Make it a meal with Meadow Muffin Soda Bread (page 150) and a light green salad.*

8 or more servings

The Beef
2 pounds stew beef, cut in bite-sized cubes
1 medium onion, sliced
1½ cups apple cider or apple juice
1 tablespoon molasses
2 cloves garlic
1 bay leaf
⅛ teaspoon ground allspice
1 tablespoon flour
Salt and pepper
2 tablespoons canola oil

The Vegetables
> 1 purple-top turnip, pared and cut into ¾" cubes (about 2 cups)
> 2 carrots, cut in 1" pieces
> 4 ribs celery, cut in 1" pieces
> 3 potatoes, cut in 1" cubes (about 1 pound)
> 1 (15-ounce) can diced tomatoes (with juice)
> 2 teaspoons lemon juice
> 2 teaspoons Worcestershire sauce
> 1 teaspoon salt
> ½ teaspoon pepper
> 1 teaspoon paprika
> 1 teaspoon sugar

1. Mix the beef cubes and onion in a large bowl. Stir the cider, molasses, garlic cloves, bay leaf and allspice together and pour over the beef and onion. Cover and refrigerate for 6 hours or overnight.

2. Remove the beef cubes from the marinade and pat dry with paper towels. Discard the garlic cloves and bay leaf. Reserve the rest of the marinade. Dust the beef cubes with the flour, some salt and pepper, and brown in hot oil in a heavy kettle or Dutch oven.

3. Pour the reserved marinade over the beef, adding a little water if necessary to just barely cover the meat. Simmer, tightly covered, over low heat, for two hours, or until the meat is very tender.

Meanwhile, proceed with the veggies.

4. Combine all of the vegetables and seasonings in a large pot. Add 8 cups water and simmer until vegetables are just barely tender, about 20 to 30 minutes.

5. Add the vegetables to the meat or vice versa, including the cooking liquid. Simmer for a few minutes more to blend the flavors.

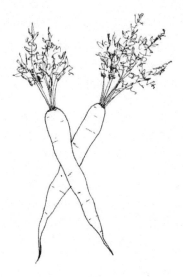

Henrietta's Recipes

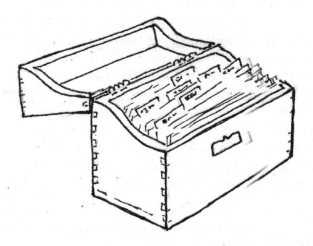

I cherish the simple wooden file box where my grandmother kept her recipes. Almost all of the recipes are in her handwriting. My grandmother, Henrietta, passed away in 1989, but memories of her come back vividly when I see her own handwriting.

Going through Gram's recipe file, I find that most of the recipes are devoted to cookies, cakes and other sweets. Why is this? She was as skinny as a rail! Also, she always baked the same cookies for us; frosted shortbread with a walnut on the top. Many of her recipes don't have titles. Sometimes you can tell what they are from the list of ingredients, but there are no prep instructions and often no baking or cooking instructions. You can guess at some things, but a lot was just understood. I imagine Gram, sitting in her kitchen, drinking tea, and chatting with her friend who had brought her something sweet. If she liked it, she asked her friend what was in it. And she wrote it down.

Even though there were divider cards in the file box, Henrietta's recipes were all just filed together in the front of the box. It is interesting to see what the dividers were, back then. No beef, poultry, seafood or beverages. However, there were separate dividers for pickles, preserves, cereals and ices. How many recipes do people have nowadays for ice cream or pickles??? Gram never referred to them as recipes, rather as "receipts."

The most endearing recipe I found in her box is one for "Viche Sois" (sic). When I was home from college, sometime in the early 60's, Mum and her sister, Judy, had become alarmed that Gram wasn't eating well. Everything that tasted good she claimed upset her stomach, or some other excuse. Basically she was living on scotch and Chesterfields. I gambled that she wouldn't turn up her nose at something made by her granddaughter, another generation removed from the daughters who were always nagging her. So I went to her house and made vichyssoise. She ate some, probably not much, but made a big fuss over my effort just the same. Going through her recipe box I found, in Gram's handwriting, the recipe for "Viche Sois." It brought tears to my eyes to realize that she sat there and wrote down what I was doing, and filed it away with her recipes.

Oh, by the way, vichyssoise is the only recipe Gram filed under "vegetables." I guess that preparing vegetables was so simple that anyone could do it without directions.

Thurber and Henrietta

Vichyssoise

The soup that I served my grandmother!

6 servings

4 tablespoons unsalted butter
4 thinly sliced leeks (white part only)
1 teaspoon salt
¼ teaspoon ground white pepper
1½ pounds russet or all-purpose potatoes (3 to 4 potatoes), peeled and
  thinly sliced
4 cups low-sodium chicken stock
1½ cups heavy cream
1 cup milk
2 tablespoons chopped fresh chives

1. Melt the butter in a soup pot over medium heat. Add the leeks and season with salt and pepper. Cook, stirring occasionally, until the leeks are tender and fragrant, but not brown, about 5 minutes.

2. Add the potatoes and the chicken stock. Bring to a boil, reduce the heat, and simmer, partially covered, until the potatoes are very tender, about 20 minutes.

3. Cool the soup until it can be safely pureed without splattering yourself with hot soup. Puree in batches in a blender or food processor. You may also use an immersion blender.

4. Return the soup to the pot. Stir in 1 cup of cream and the milk and bring to a simmer over medium heat. Season with more salt and pepper and cook for a minute or two. Cover, cool, and then chill thoroughly.

5. Stir in the remaining ½ cup cream just before serving. Sprinkle each serving with chives.

Part 7: Around The County

Various Cultures

French

> Tourtiere* (Pork Pie)
> Poutine (OMG Fries)
> Patate Fricassee* (Beef Stew with Spuds)
> Soupe aux Pois (Split Pea Soup)
> Rappie Pie (Chicken and Grated Spuds)

Lebanese or Syrian

> Syrian Potato Salad

Swedish

> Hasselback Potato Fans
> Swedish New Potatoes
> Hot Potato Salad

Native American

> Fiddleheads

* We Mainers prefer the Acadian spelling (no accent) to the (snooty) Parisien spelling. Tourtiere and fricassee taste just as good as—maybe better than— tourtière and fricassée.

Various Cultures

Aroostook County is home to quite a few distinct cultures in addition to the Scotch-Irish people of my own heritage. There were many French descendants, in fact about half of the population of my little town. Other towns, just to the north, were almost all French. I heard French spoken often, in the fields, about town, and in the homes of many friends. Not in school though! English was considered the language of choice. French was taught in the high school, but there was a bias toward "Parisien" French. My friends from French families had a nice advantage in French class!

The French people up north, and across the border in Quebec, love their poutine. While you may enjoy a hearty squirt of ketchup with your French fries, you haven't lived (or died!), until you have tried poutine; fries smothered in cheese curds and gravy. We jokingly call poutine a "heart attack on a plate." A favorite Christmas Eve treat is Tourtiere; ground pork and potato pie, equally heavy, and mighty delicious!

There were several Syrian families in Fort Fairfield and Caribou, and they lent an exotic air to the regional cooking. These families emigrated to northern Maine in the 1890's to escape religious persecution in what is now Lebanon. My parents were good friends with the several Syrian families. We often enjoyed sandwiches in Syrian bread (now commonly available as pita bread), and we loved kibbee (raw beefsteak, heavily seasoned) and tabbouleh. The Syrians also liked to add fresh mint to their salads.

A good-sized Swedish colony was established in the 1870's just north of Caribou. After the Civil War many young men heeded the call to "go West." The Swedish families were recruited to help fill the population gap left by the western pioneers. Many of their descendants still live in New Sweden and Stockholm, Maine.

Northern Maine is home to many Native Americans, although the nearest reservation is just across the border in New Brunswick. Micmacs and Maliseets are two federally recognized tribes that have bands living in Aroostook County. The food I most associate with my Indian friends is fiddleheads.

Tourtiere (Pork Pie)

This meat pie is a Christmas Eve tradition in Franco-American households.

Helpful Hint: *I have heard of people saving time by using instant potatoes in this dish. Go ahead and try it that way! I won't tell! You could also use ready-made refrigerated pie crusts.*

6 servings

2 or 3 all-purpose potatoes
1½ pounds ground pork (or ¾ pound ground pork and ¾ pound ground beef)
1 cup minced onion
1 clove garlic, minced
½ teaspoon salt
½ teaspoon freshly ground black pepper
¼ teaspoon ground cloves
¼ teaspoon ground allspice
½ cup water (or ¼ cup dry red wine and ¼ cup water)
1 recipe pastry for a 9", double-crust, deep-dish pie

1. Peel the potatoes and cut into chunks. Boil until soft, 15 to 20 minutes. Drain and mash well.

2. Put the ground meat in a very large skillet. Add the onion and garlic. Cook, breaking up the meat with a spatula, until no longer red. Spoon off excess grease. Add salt, pepper, cloves, and allspice. Stir to combine.

3. Add the water (and optional wine) to the skillet and bring to a simmer. Gradually stir in the mashed potato. Simmer until the liquid is reduced and the mixture is thickened, about 10 minutes.

Preheat the oven to 350°.

4. Prepare your pastry while the filling is thickening.

5. Line a 9" pie plate with pastry. Spoon in the filling, spreading evenly. Cover with the top crust and crimp the top and bottom crusts together. Cut several slits to ventilate. Be creative! Make it beautiful!

6. Bake the tourtiere for 50 minutes at 350°. If the edges brown too fast, cover the edges with a strip of foil.

Bon appétit! Joyeux Noel!

Poutine (OMG Fries)

A Franco-American (also Canadian) take on French fries!

Helpful Hint: *Russet, long white potatoes, and round yellow potatoes work well in this recipe.*

4 to 8 servings, but who's counting?

6 to 8 large potatoes (about 2 pounds)
The Gravy
    1 tablespoon vegetable oil
    1 small onion, minced
    1 clove garlic, minced
    1 (15-ounce) can chicken broth
    1 (15-ounce) can beef broth
    2 tablespoons ketchup
    1 tablespoon cider vinegar
    ½ teaspoon Worcestershire sauce
    ½ teaspoon soy sauce
    2 tablespoons butter
    2 tablespoons flour
    1 teaspoon salt
    ½ teaspoon pepper
Vegetable oil for frying
2 cups cheddar cheese curds

1. Peel the potatoes and slice lengthwise, about ¼" thick. Stack the slices and cut lengthwise into ¼"-thick sticks. Place in a large bowl filled with ice water and let sit at least 1 hour.

2. Meanwhile, make the gravy. Heat 1 tablespoon vegetable oil in a saucepan. Add the onion and garlic and sauté until translucent, about 2 minutes. Add the chicken and beef broth, ketchup, vinegar, Worcestershire sauce and soy sauce. Bring to a boil.

3. In a separate saucepan, melt the butter over medium heat. Add the flour and make a roux, stirring for about 1 minute. Whisk the stock mixture into the roux and simmer until reduced by half, about 20 minutes. Strain the gravy, season with salt and pepper and keep warm.

Now back to the potatoes.

4. Drain and pat the potato slices dry. Heat the oil in a heavy-bottomed pot or deep-fryer to 350°. Fry the potatoes in small batches until whitish-yellow, about 8 minutes. Drain on paper towels. Bring the temperature of the oil up to 375°. Fry the potatoes in batches again until golden brown, about 6 to 8 minutes. Drain on fresh paper towels. Salt and pepper the fries while hot.

5. Put the fries in shallow bowls and top with cheese curds and gravy.

I will not kid you, the easiest thing to do is buy a bag of freezer-aisle French fries and heat them in the oven. The gravy is important, though. The canned stuff will not work! Yuk!!

> **Surgeon General's Warning: A regular diet of
> Poutine could be hazardous to your health!**

Patate Fricassee (Beef Stew with Spuds)

The Bouchard Family Farm of Fort Kent is well known for their buckwheat ployes (pancakes). In addition to buckwheat they also grow potatoes. My friend, Jane, is a member of that family. She would have served a stack of ployes with Patate Fricassee to soak up the yummy gravy. This recipe is adapted from the Bouchard Family Farm's **French Acadian Cookbook.**

Helpful Hint*: Ployes mix can be found in many supermarkets, often in the ethnic foods section.*

4 to 5 servings

1½ pounds beef round steak
Salt and freshly ground pepper
2 tablespoons vegetable oil
1 medium onion, roughly chopped
2 cloves garlic, minced
3 beef bouillon cubes
1 to 2 cups hot water
4 potatoes, peeled and sliced (about 3 cups)

1. Cut the meat into 1" cubes. Sprinkle with salt and pepper.

2. Heat the oil in a heavy, deep skillet. Add the beef cubes and brown on all sides. Add the onion and garlic and sauté until translucent.

3. Dissolve the bouillon cubes in boiling water and pour over the beef cubes. Add more hot water to just cover the meat. Cover and simmer until meat is tender, about 20 to 30 minutes.

4. Add the potatoes, cover and simmer another 20 minutes, until the potatoes are tender. Add more hot water or broth, if necessary, so the mixture doesn't get dry.

5. Serve with ployes if you can. Or a baguette! Or biscuits, page 153.

Soupe aux Pois (Split Pea Soup)

Franco-American comfort food!

Helpful Hint: *A potato helps to bind the soup and keep it from separating.*

8 servings

2 cups yellow split peas (about 1 pound)
7 cups water, divided
2 tablespoons butter
1 medium onion, chopped
1 cup diced carrots
1 cup diced celery
1 clove garlic, minced
1 medium russet potato, peeled and cut in ½" dice
1 meaty ham bone (alternately ½ pound ham, cut in small chunks)
3 bay leaves
¼ teaspoon thyme
1 teaspoon salt, or more, to taste
Freshly ground pepper to taste
2 tablespoons cider vinegar or white wine, optional

1. Combine the peas and 6 cups of water in a large heavy pot or a slow cooker. Bring to a boil and reduce heat to a slow simmer.

2. Meanwhile, melt the butter in a large skillet. Add the onion, carrots, celery, and garlic. Cook, stirring frequently, until the vegetables are softened, about 4 to 5 minutes.

3. Add the potato to the skillet, along with the remaining cup of water. Cover and cook for 5 minutes, or until the potato is soft.

4. Add the vegetables from the skillet to the pot or the slow cooker. Add the ham bone or ham chunks, bay leaves, thyme, salt and pepper.

5. Simmer the soup until the peas are soft and mushy, about 1½ hours (3 hours, if using a slow cooker). Add more water if the soup becomes too thick before the peas are thoroughly cooked and soft. Add the cider vinegar or white wine, if desired, during the last 15 minutes. Remove bay leaves. Taste and adjust seasonings before serving.

Rappie Pie (Chicken and Grated Spuds)

Rappie Pie is a well-known Acadian dish from Nova Scotia. The name comes from the French word "rapure," meaning " grated."

In the 1700's, when the British drove out the French people from Nova Scotia, many families resettled in Louisiana. Others made their way up the St. John River into French Canada, and in 1785 settled along the St. John River Valley. Those on the southern side of the river became Americans in 1840 when the border between Maine and Canada was drawn. The connecting bonds between the Cajuns in Louisiana, the Acadian French people in Northern Maine, and the Acadians who stayed on in Nova Scotia are very strong.

While Nova Scotia is not actually part of Northern Maine, and not even geographically adjacent, we feel the cultural connection. Like many potato recipes, Rappie Pie is intended to feed a crowd.

Helpful Hint*: This will take all day! (Now, that was helpful!) You will need a very large stock pot for the chicken, a very large bowl for mixing, and a 10" by 14" baking pan.*

12 or more servings

1 whole chicken, 5 or 6 pounds
2 medium onions, chopped
5 chicken bouillon cubes or 2 tablespoons bouillon paste
Salt and black pepper, as needed
5 quarts water
4 ounces salt pork
10-pound bag of potatoes
Butter (to grease the pan)

1. Cut the chicken in pieces. Place in a very large stock pot and cover with 5 quarts of water. Add the chopped onions, bouillon cubes or paste, salt and black pepper. (Keep in mind that the bouillon cubes or paste is quite salty.) Simmer for 2 hours.

2. Cut the salt pork in ¼" dice, fry until crisp, drain on paper towels, and set aside.

3. Peel, wash and grate the potatoes. Squeeze potatoes dry in a cheesecloth bag (about 2 cups at a time). Ten pounds of potatoes should yield 4 to 5 pounds of grated potatoes.

4. Save the broth from the cooked chicken. Shred and set aside the cooked and cooled chicken. Discard the skin and bones.

5. Place the grated potato pulp in a large bowl. Loosen it up and add boiling broth from the chicken, gradually, about 2 cups at a time. Eventually you should have about as much potato mixture as before the potatoes were squeezed. Add salt and pepper to taste.

6. Grease the baking pan with butter. Pour half of the potato mixture into the pan and spread evenly. Distribute the shredded chicken evenly over this and cover with the other half of the potato mixture. Sprinkle the crisp salt pork bits evenly over the top.

7. Bake at 450° for 1 hour. Lower the heat to 400, and cook 2 more hours.

8. Cut in 12 or more squares and serve with condiments of your choice. Typical options include pickles, butter, molasses, and, of course, ketchup.

RAPPIE PIE

5 or 6 lb. fowl or chicken, quite fat
2/3 pail big potatoes
2 medium onions
salt and pepper

The Original Recipe

Syrian Potato Salad

This recipe would have been served by our Aroostook County Syrian friends.

Helpful Hint: *Round red or white potatoes are best for potato salad.*

6 servings

6 medium red or white potatoes (about 2 pounds)
The Dressing:
    ⅓ cup extra virgin olive oil
    ¼ cup freshly squeezed lemon juice
    1 clove garlic, minced
    ½ teaspoon salt
    ¼ teaspoon pepper
The Salad:
    ⅓ cup finely snipped parsley
    ⅓ cup finely snipped fresh mint
    6 scallions, green part only, snipped
Garnishes:
    Cherry tomatoes
    Kalamata olives

1. Scrub or peel the potatoes. Cut them in quarters and boil for 20 minutes, until soft. Drain the potatoes and allow them to cool.

2. Whisk the dressing ingredients together in a small bowl.

3. Slice or cube the cooled potatoes. Place in a large bowl. Add the parsley, mint and scallions. Toss to combine.

4. Pour half of the dressing over the salad and toss. Continue to add dressing to the salad until you like the consistency.

5. Mound the salad on a serving platter and decorate with your choice of garnishes.

Hasselback Potato Fans

A Swedish specialty! Crunchy and delicious!

> 1 medium potato per person. If they are very large, each potato will yield
> 2 servings.

> For <u>each</u> potato:
> 1 tablespoon butter, melted
> Salt and pepper
> 2 teaspoons grated Cheddar cheese
> 1 teaspoon fine breadcrumbs

Preheat oven at 425°.

1. Scrub potatoes. Cutting almost all the way through, slice each potato across in very thin (⅛") slivers, leaving the potato slivers attached at the bottom. Arrange in a baking dish and fan out the slices slightly.

2. Drizzle each potato with half of the melted butter. Sprinkle with salt and pepper.

3. Bake at 425° for 35 to 40 minutes.

4. Drizzle each potato with the remaining butter. Sprinkle with the grated cheese and breadcrumbs.

5. Bake 20 minutes more.

Swedish New Potatoes

Very small "new" potatoes can often be found at any time of the year. The tastiest ones were dug just this morning!

Helpful Hint: *This dish can be served hot, cold, or at room temperature.*

Helpful Hint #2: *If you have leftover dressing, it is delicious on a tossed green salad.*

6 to 8 servings

2 pounds very small new potatoes
The Dressing:
 ¼ cup extra virgin olive oil
 ¼ cup canola oil
 ¼ cup white wine vinegar
 1 tablespoon Dijon mustard
 1 clove garlic, minced
 ¼ teaspoon salt
 ⅛ teaspoon pepper
 1 tablespoon sugar
 Pinch of dried dill
The salad:
 2 tablespoons capers, rinsed
 ¼ cup dill pickle relish
 Salt and pepper
 Fresh dill

1. Wash the potatoes gently, but do not peel. Boil in salted water for 10 to 15 minutes, until just barely soft.

2. While the potatoes are cooking, whisk the dressing ingredients together in a small bowl.

3. Drain the potatoes and return them to the pot.

4. Pour half of the dressing over the still-hot potatoes. Mix in the capers and relish. Season with salt and pepper and add more dressing to taste.

5. Garnish with snipped fresh dill before serving.

Charlie and Fred

Hot Potato Salad

I first had hot potato salad when it was served by my friend Ellen, who grew up in New Sweden, Maine.

Helpful Hint: *All-purpose white potatoes are best for this dish.*

6 servings

4 to 5 medium white potatoes (about 1½ pounds)
The Dressing:
    ½ cup mayonnaise
    ½ cup plain yogurt
    1 tablespoon cider vinegar
    1 teaspoon Dijon mustard
    1 tablespoon sugar
    ½ teaspoon salt
    ¼ teaspoon pepper
½ cup minced red onion
Parsley, snipped, for garnish

1. Scrub or peel the potatoes. Cut them in quarters and boil for 20 minutes, until soft.

2. While the potatoes are cooking, whisk the dressing ingredients together in a small bowl.

3. Drain the potatoes and return them to the pot.

4. Pour half of the dressing over the still-hot potatoes and mash with a potato masher or a hand mixer. Continue to add dressing to the potatoes until you like the consistency. Mix in the minced onion.

5. Keep the potatoes warm in a very low oven until serving time. Garnish with snipped parsley just before serving.

Fiddleheads

You have to know where to find fiddleheads, along the low-lying banks of certain streams and rivers, in late May. Or be lucky enough to have a Native American (First Nation) friend who will bring you some! Don't count on them showing you where they were found. Those spots are usually closely guarded secrets.

In season, you may be able to find fresh fiddleheads in gourmet markets.

4 to 6 servings

4 cups fiddlehead ferns, cleaned and rinsed thoroughly
1 tablespoon butter
Cider vinegar to serve

1. Brush off the thin brown membrane flakes, and break off the stems, leaving about 2 to 3" of stem. Wash gently.

2. Bring a pot of salted water to a boil. Add fiddleheads and cook until just tender, about 5 minutes. Drain.

3. Season with butter, salt and pepper. Serve warm in individual bowls and pass the vinegar.

Part 8: Around the World

Irish Staple

Colcannon (Mashed with Kale or Cabbage)
Bangers and Mash (Sausages)

1965 Liverpool, England

England - Fish and Chips (Fries)
Scotland - Finnan Haddie (Haddock)
Spain - Roberto's Tortilla (Spanish Omelet)
France - Potatoes Parmentier
Italy - Florentine Frittata (Baked Omelet)
Eastern Europe - Classic Potato Latkes (Grated Potato Pancakes)
Germany - German Potato Salad
Sweden - Janssen's Temptation (Scalloped, with Anchovies)
Denmark - Danish Browned Potatoes
Russia - Solyanka (Potato and Cabbage)
China - Spicy Chinese Potatoes
Australia - Australian Stuffed Spuds
Peru - Peruvian Roasted Potatoes
Mexico
    Nopalitos con Papas (Cactus Paddles with Potatoes)
    Mexican Roasted Potatoes
New Mexico USA
    Green Chile Stew
    Breakfast Burritos

Irish Staple

Potatoes are the food staple that has saved many cultures from starvation. The Irish, of course, are the most famous. The Irish were a sorry lot of people before the potato came along. Their island produced barely enough wheat to keep the natives from starvation, and their English landlords kept or exported most of the best wheat for themselves. In addition, wheat had to be milled before it could be baked into nourishment. The potato, on the other hand, simply had to be boiled or baked. When you add milk you have a complete protein. Most poor Irish farmers had a cow or two, so with the introduction of the potato they became far less dependent on the English and their mills. Mashed potatoes with added milk equals the perfect food. And the potato is ridiculously easy to grow. Cut them up, stick them in the ground, and they will grow.

The potato arrived in Ireland in about 1600, and by 1800 it was the principal food—and sometimes the only food—for over a million people. The population of poor Irish tenant farmers doubled in the years after the introduction of the potato.

When the potato blight arrived in Ireland in 1847 it devastated the entire crop. Poor tenant farmers, whose families subsisted almost exclusively on potatoes, watched their whole source of food disappear within days. During the Great Famine of 1847 to 1852, nearly 15 percent of the population died from starvation. Those who were able made their way to America. They were desperate, ragged, poor and malnourished, but they were the strong ones, the lucky ones.

I am not sure when my grandparents or their parents immigrated to the Boston area. It does seem fairly certain that both the McGee family (grandfather Thomas James McGee) and the Sweeney family (grandmother Katherine Sweeney) came from County Donegal. I visited Donegal in 1965 while on a hitch-hiking adventure with a friend. We found that a branch of the McGee family had become quite successful in apparel retailing ("McGee of Donegal"). I found some Sweeneys in the countryside who were less gentrified and more open to American relatives on a hunt for their roots. I chose to buy my hand knitted Aran sweater from them.

The Irish roots are deep and strong, especially in our imagination.

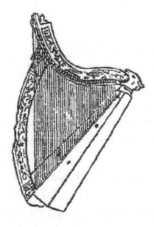

The Irish love colcannon so much they sing a song about it!

Did you ever eat colcannon
Made with lovely pickled cream,
With the greens & scallions mingled
Like a picture in a dream?
Did you ever make a hole on top
To hold the melting flake
Or the creamy flavored butter
That your mother used to make?

CHORUS:
Yes, you did, so you did,
So did he and so did I,
And the more I think about it
Sure the nearer I'm to cry.
Oh wasn't it the happy days
When troubles we had not,
And our mothers made colcannon
In the little skillet pot?

Colcannon (Mashed with Kale or Cabbage)

Helpful Hint: You can substitute 2 cups of shredded cabbage for the kale.

6 servings

4 medium potatoes (about 1½ pounds)
½ cup milk
2 tablespoons butter, divided
1 teaspoon salt
Freshly ground pepper to taste
3 cups chopped kale
6 green onions or scallions, chopped
1 tablespoon snipped parsley
Grated cheddar, optional

Preheat the oven to 400°.

1. Cut the potatoes into 2" cubes and boil in salted water until tender. Drain and return to the pot. Mash with the milk and 1 tablespoon of the butter.

2. Melt the remaining butter in a large frying pan. Add the kale and green onions and sauté until the kale has wilted and the onion is translucent, about 3 minutes.

3. Combine the kale and onion with the mashed potatoes. Season with the salt and pepper. Stir in the parsley.

4. Spoon into a casserole dish and bake for 15 to 20 minutes. Sprinkle with grated cheddar for the last 5 minutes if desired.

Bangers and Mash (Sausages)

More English and Irish comfort food! Bangers (sausages) got their name because of their tendency to burst (bang!) while cooking. I loved this supper when I was in Liverpool during my college days.

Helpful Hint: This dish is not complete without the onion gravy.

4 servings

For the gravy:
   1 medium onion (about ½ pound), peeled and thinly sliced
   1 tablespoon vegetable oil
   1 tablespoon butter
   1 15-ounce can low-sodium beef broth
   ½ cup dry red wine
   2 teaspoons corn starch
   2 tablespoons cold water
   Salt and freshly ground black pepper, to taste
For the mash:
   4 medium potatoes (about 1½ pounds) peeled and cut in chunks
   ½ cup milk
   2 tablespoons butter
   Salt and pepper, to taste
Bangers:
   8 links pork or beef sausage
   Oil for the pan

Start the onion gravy first:

1. Melt the oil and butter together in a large skillet. Add the onion and stir to combine. Cover with a lid and cook over low heat for 8 to 10 minutes, stirring occasionally.

2. Pour in the beef broth and red wine. Boil gently, uncovered, for 5 minutes.

3. Stir the cornstarch and cold water together in a small bowl. Pour in a little of the hot gravy and mix thoroughly. Add the cornstarch mixture to the gravy in the skillet and mix thoroughly.

4. Cook 5 minutes more, until the gravy is slightly thickened. Season with salt and pepper to taste. Keep warm while you prepare the sausages and mashed potatoes.

Start the potatoes while the gravy is cooking.

5. Boil the potatoes in enough salted water to cover them until they can be easily pierced with a fork (about 20 minutes).

6. Drain the potatoes and return them to the pot. Shake the pot over low heat until the excess water has evaporated.

7. Add the milk and butter to the pot. Keep the burner on low for a few seconds more, until the butter has melted and the milk has warmed. Be careful not to boil the milk, which will make it curdle. (Alternately, warm the milk and butter together in the microwave.)

8. Remove the pot from the heat. Use a potato masher to mash to the consistency you like.

Prepare the sausages:

9. While the potatoes are cooking, heat a little oil in a frying pan. Fry the sausages until they are browned on all sides. Keep warm until you are ready to serve.

Spoon the mash onto 4 dinner plates. Top each serving with 2 bangers. Pass the onion gravy to pour over each serving.

1965 Liverpool, England

When I arrived in Liverpool in the summer of 1965, I was immediately asked two questions by my new acquaintances. First, "Who do you fancy, the Beatles or the Stones?" And second, "Who are you for, Liverpool or Everton?" The first question was easy to answer. I loved them both! The second question had me stumped. The Liverpool and Everton football clubs (soccer teams, to us Americans) were locked in a fierce rivalry, and both were in World Cup contention that year.

I went to Liverpool as a Winant Volunteer, an exchange program for young Brits and Americans. Originally conceived as a way for American youth to help with the clean-up and rebuilding effort in Britain after World War II, the program had developed into a social work exchange. My assignment for the summer was to assist the director of Bankfield House, the Garston Parish Youth Club.

I lived at University Settlement on Nile Street, along with two other American college girls who were also Winant Volunteers. There were two young British women who shared the second floor with us, and five British lads who lived on the third floor. All of them were studying social work at the University.

University Settlement was an old hotel that had been repurposed as a dorm. There was a cook who came in five nights a week to prepare an evening meal which was called "high tea." It was a more substantial meal than "tea," which usually happened at about 4:00 in the afternoon, and might include some "biscuits" (cookies) along with the tea. High tea was more like a light supper, with tea, of course.

My day at Bankfield House began in early afternoon, and ran into the evening most days. I often missed high tea. By the time I got home I was tired and hungry. My habit was to stop at the neighborhood "chippie," just across the street, for fish and chips.

You have read this far. You know there is a potato in this story somewhere! "Chips" are French fries, although they might not be cut in such regular strips. "Crisps" are what we think of as potato chips.

Traditionally fish and chips were served in a cone made from a rolled up piece of newspaper. Chips went in first, followed by a chunk of fried fish, and the whole thing sprinkled very generously with salt and malt vinegar. If some of the newsprint smeared off onto your snack, well so much the better! My British friends used to claim they could tell which newspaper they were eating from by the taste of the newsprint. (My favorite newspaper was the Manchester Guardian. I loved that paper so much that I continued to subscribe to the overseas edition for several years.)

I had a heck of a time finding malt vinegar when I first got back to the US. Luckily, there are many kinds of vinegar available today and malt vinegar is not hard to find.

You were expecting a recipe, right? Well here it is!

Fish and Chips (Fries)

The original street food! In England, chips are what we call "French Fries." Potato chips are called "crisps."

Helpful Hint: *Fresh cod or haddock will be most authentic in this recipe.*

6 servings

Good-quality cooking oil
The Batter
  1½ cups all-purpose flour
  1 teaspoon baking soda
  Salt and pepper
  1 (12 ounce) bottle beer
  Malt vinegar
1½ pounds fresh cod or haddock fillets
6 medium potatoes
Extra flour
More salt and more malt vinegar

1. Heat cooking oil in a deep fat fryer to 375°.

2. Make the batter. Put flour, soda, salt and pepper in a large bowl. Add the beer gradually (about half of a 12-ounce bottle), stopping when you have a thick batter. Whisk thoroughly until there are no lumps. Add a splash (1 tablespoon) of malt vinegar and set aside.

3. Peel the potatoes and cut into chunky chips. Rinse in cold water and dry thoroughly.

4. Fry chips in the hot oil for about 3 minutes, until soft but not browned. Drain and set to one side on a plate lined with paper towels.

5. Adjust the temperature in the fryer to 350°.

6. Put some flour onto a plate. Dredge the fish fillet in the flour.

7. Dip each fish fillet in the batter and swirl until thoroughly coated.

8. Fry the fish fillets in the hot oil for 6 to 8 minutes, depending on the thickness of the fish. Keep warm in the oven on a tray lined with paper towels.

9. Turn the temperature in the fryer back up to 375°. Fry the chips again for 1 to 2 minutes, until they are golden and crisp.

10. Serve fish and chips wrapped in a cone made of newsprint (very authentic!), or on plates. Sprinkle generously with salt and malt vinegar.

"Ferry 'cross the Mersey" 1965

Finnan Haddie (Haddock)

Comfort food with Scottish origins!

Helpful Hint: *Finnan Haddie is lightly smoked haddock, and should be treated like fresh fish, that is, consumed within three days.*

6 servings

1½ pounds Finnan Haddie
1 bay leaf
1 small onion, sliced thin
Pinch thyme
2 to 3 cups milk
¼ cup butter
¼ cup flour
⅛ teaspoon nutmeg
2 hard boiled eggs
Freshly ground pepper to taste
6 medium potatoes, about 2 pounds, peeled, boiled and mashed (page 12)
1 tablespoon snipped parsley

1. Place the fish in a wide pan, add the bay leaf, sliced onion, thyme and enough milk to cover everything. Soak for 1 hour.

2. Place the pan over very low heat and simmer for 10 to 20 minutes, depending on the thickness of the fish.

3. Meanwhile, melt the butter in the top of a double boiler or in a heavy pan. Blend in the flour and cook and stir over low heat for 1 minute. Gradually stir in 1 cup of fresh milk and 1 cup of the cooking liquid. Remove the bay leaf, but keep the onion if you wish. Continue to cook and stir until the sauce has thickened. Add the nutmeg and freshly ground pepper to taste.

4. Flake the fish, and chop the eggs. Add the fish and the eggs to the sauce and heat through. Thin with more milk, if desired, and season with pepper to taste.

5. Serve over mashed potatoes and sprinkle with parsley.

Note: *Serve over simple boiled potatoes if you wish.*

Roberto's Tortilla (Spanish Omelet)

Roberto says this tortilla is often served as tapas, a light snack to go with drinks at the end of the afternoon. I think it makes an excellent supper dish or filling for a sandwich. The potatoes are traditionally deep-fried in olive oil in an oven-going skillet.

Helpful Hint: *This works best using a non-stick, 10" skillet with a handle that can take the heat. A cast iron skillet works well if it is well seasoned.*

4 to 6 servings

4 tablespoons olive oil, divided
1 small onion, cut in very thin wedges (about 1 cup)
2 medium russet potatoes (about 1 pound), peeled and sliced very thin (⅛")
5 large eggs
1 teaspoon salt
¼ teaspoon freshly ground pepper

1. Heat 1 tablespoon of the olive oil in an oven-going skillet. Add the onion wedges. Cook and stir until translucent, but not browned. Remove to a small bowl.

2. Add the remaining 3 tablespoons olive oil to the skillet. When hot, add the potato slices. Cook until the potatoes are very tender and have started to brown at the edges. Turn the potatoes with a spatula occasionally to be sure they are coking evenly.

3. Meanwhile, beat the eggs in a medium bowl. Add the salt and pepper.

4. Add the onions to the potatoes in the skillet and mix to combine. Pour the eggs over the potato mixture.

Preheat the broiler after step 4.

5. Cook the egg and potatoes over medium heat, shaking the pan occasionally and loosening the sides with a spatula, until the edges begin to brown, about 5 minutes. Place the skillet 5" to 7" under a broiler for a minute or two (watch carefully!) to completely set the eggs.

6. Invert onto a plate and cut into wedges to serve.

Helpful Hint #2: *Although this dish is traditionally inverted onto a plate to serve, my inversion skills are not perfect. I have been known to serve it directly out of the skillet.*

Potatoes Parmentier

Antoine-Augustin Parmentier (1787 – 1813) was a French chemist and nutritionist. He championed the humble potato as a food source in France and throughout Europe. This is a classic French presentation.

Helpful Hint: *You can use olive oil in place of the butter if you prefer.*

4 to 6 servings

2 pounds potatoes, unpeeled, scrubbed, and cut into ½" cubes
1 teaspoon salt
2 cloves garlic, lightly crushed
3 tablespoons melted butter, divided
2 tablespoons chopped flat-leaf parsley
2 tablespoons chopped cilantro
2 tablespoons chopped mint
½ teaspoon lemon zest
1 teaspoon lemon juice
Salt and freshly ground black pepper, to taste

Preheat the oven to 400°

1. Parboil the potatoes in a saucepan with 1 teaspoon salt and the crushed garlic for about 2 minutes. Drain, remove the garlic cloves, and return the potatoes to the pot. Dry out the potatoes by shaking the pot over very low heat.

2. Toss the potato cubes with 2 tablespoons of the melted butter. Spread the potato cubes on a baking tray and roast in the oven until golden and crispy, about 30 minutes. Toss once or twice while roasting.

3. Mix the parsley, cilantro, mint, lemon zest and lemon juice with the remaining 1 tablespoon of the melted butter. Toss with the potatoes. Add salt and freshly ground black pepper to taste.

Florentine Frittata (Baked Omelet)

An Italian supper dish!

Helpful Hint: *Use a large cast iron skillet if you have one.*

4 to 6 servings

6 large eggs
½ teaspoon dried basil
½ teaspoon dried oregano
½ teaspoon salt
Freshly ground black pepper
4 slices bacon, chopped
2 medium white potatoes, peeled and cut in ½" dice (about 8 ounces)
2 tablespoons olive oil, divided
½ cup roughly chopped onion
1 clove garlic, minced
1 small bunch spinach or arugula, coarsely chopped
4 slices provolone or mozzarella cheese
2 tablespoons grated parmesan

1. Whisk together the eggs, basil, oregano, salt and pepper. Set aside.

2. In a 9" or 10" oven-going skillet, cook the bacon until crisp. Transfer the bacon to a large bowl and pour off all but 2 tablespoons of the fat.

3. Add the potatoes to the skillet and sauté until the potatoes just start to turn golden. Add 1 tablespoon olive oil, if needed. Add the onion and garlic and continue to sauté until the onion is translucent. Add the spinach or arugula and sauté just until wilted.

4. Pour the vegetables into the bowl with the reserved bacon and stir gently to mix.

Preheat the broiler.

5. Add the remaining tablespoon olive oil to the skillet. When hot, return the vegetable mixture to the skillet, spreading evenly.

6. Pour the egg mixture evenly over the vegetables and cook over medium heat, lifting the edges with a spatula, and letting the uncooked egg flow underneath, about 2 minutes. Lower the heat, cover the skillet and cook until the egg appears almost set.

7. Uncover the skillet and top the frittata with the provolone or mozzarella. Sprinkle with the grated parmesan. Broil the frittata 5" to 7" from the heat until the cheese is melted, 1 or 2 minutes. Watch carefully!

8. Cut into wedges to serve.

Sicilian variation: Omit bacon. Substitute 2 tablespoons olive oil for the bacon fat. Substitute ½ cup chopped sweet red pepper and 2 cups chopped broccoli florets, lightly steamed, for the spinach or arugula.

Classic Potato Latkes (Grated Potato Pancakes)

These are traditionally served during the Hanukkah holiday.

Helpful Hint: *You can keep the latkes warm in a 200° oven for up to 1 hour.*

6 to 8 servings

6 medium russet potatoes (about 2 pounds)
1 small onion, finely chopped
1 tablespoon potato starch or flour
½ cup matzo meal
2 teaspoons kosher salt
¼ teaspoon freshly ground pepper
2 eggs, beaten
½ cup, or more, vegetable oil
Applesauce and/or sour cream, to serve

1. Grate the potatoes using a food processor or the large holes of a box grater.

2. Spread the grated potatoes and the chopped onion evenly over a clean kitchen towel. Roll up, jelly-roll style, and twist to squeeze out as much moisture as possible. You may have to do this in batches. Transfer the potatoes and onion to a medium bowl.

3. In a small bowl, combine the potato starch or flour, matzo meal, salt and pepper. Beat the eggs in a separate bowl.

4. Combine the potato mixture, the matzo mixture and the eggs. Form into 12 three-inch patties.

5. In a large, deep skillet, heat ⅓" of oil to 350°.

6. Fry the patties in batches of 3 or 4, for 3 to 4 minutes per side, until golden brown and crispy.

7. Transfer to a rack set over paper towels to drain the oil.

8. Serve warm, with applesauce and/or sour cream.

German Potato Salad

German potato salad is traditionally served warm.

Helpful Hint*: Round red or white potatoes are best for potato salad. Peel them or not, your choice!*

6 servings

4 to 5 medium red or white potatoes (about 1½ pounds)
The Dressing
   ¼ pound bacon, diced
   1 cup diced red onion
   ⅓ cup cider vinegar
   1 teaspoon Dijon mustard
   2 tablespoons olive oil
Salt and black pepper
¼ cup minced parsley

1. Scrub or peel the potatoes. Cut them in quarters and boil for 20 minutes, until soft. Drain the potatoes and cut in ½" dice when cool enough to handle. Keep potatoes warm.

2. Meanwhile, fry the diced bacon in a skillet until crisp. Remove with a slotted spoon to a plate lined with paper towels, reserving the bacon grease.

3. Add the diced red onion to the skillet and cook until soft and transparent.

4. Add the cider vinegar, mustard, sugar and olive oil to the skillet. Warm until sugar has dissolved.

5. Pour half of the dressing from the skillet over the warm potatoes and toss. Continue to add dressing to the salad until you like the consistency.

6. Season with salt and pepper. Sprinkle with minced parsley to serve.

Jansson's Temptation (Scalloped with Anchovies)

If you are a fan of anchovies, this Swedish specialty is for you!

Helpful Hint #1*: Long, low-temperature baking is the key. If the temperature is too high, the cream or milk will curdle.*

Helpful Hint #2*: For true anchovy lovers, reserve the liquid from the tin of anchovies. Substitute the liquid from the anchovy tin for the butter in step 4. Or add the butter, for a richer dish.*

6 servings

3 to 4 russet potatoes (about 2 pounds)
Freshly ground pepper
1 medium onion, sliced in ⅛" slices
1 (3-ounce) tin anchovy fillets, drained and chopped (reserve liquid if desired)
1 pint heavy cream (or part milk)
2 tablespoons butter

Preheat the oven to 325°.

Lightly butter a 13" x 9" x 2" glass baking dish.

1. Peel the potatoes and slice in ¼" slices. Lay the slices on their sides and slice into ¼" matchsticks.

2. Layer one-third of the potato matchsticks in the prepared baking dish. Sprinkle with pepper. Sprinkle half of the chopped onion followed by half of the anchovy fillets.

3. Repeat with another third of the potatoes and the rest of the chopped onion and anchovy fillets.

4. Top with the remaining potato matchsticks.

5. Pour the cream evenly over the potatoes. Dot with pieces of butter and sprinkle with more pepper.

6. Cover the baking dish tightly with foil. Bake for 1 hour.

7. Decrease the oven temperature to 300°. Uncover the casserole and bake for 30 to 45 minutes more. Test by dropping a knife into the potatoes to see if they are tender.

8. Remove from the oven. Let stand 15 minutes before serving.

Danish Browned Potatoes

In Denmark this dish is called Brunede Kartofler. My friend Peggy liked to make these delectable "new" potatoes. Although Peggy's father was Franco-American, her mother was Danish, and I believe that is where the recipe originated. I have seen these potatoes served as an appetizer.

Helpful Hint: *This dish can be served hot, cold, or at room temperature. It is traditional on Christmas Eve in Denmark.*

6 servings

2 pounds very small new potatoes
3 tablespoons sugar
3 tablespoons butter
1 to 2 tablespoons water, if needed

1. Wash the potatoes gently, but do not peel. Boil in salted water for 15 to 20 minutes, until just barely soft.

2. Drain the potatoes and set aside. (This step can be done in advance.)

3. Sprinkle the sugar in a cold frying pan. Heat slowly over low heat, without stirring, until the sugar has melted.

4. Add the butter and stir until you have a syrup. Turn the heat up to high and add the potatoes to the syrup. Swirl the mixture until the potatoes are nicely coated and browned. If the syrup becomes too thick, add a little water.

Russian Solyanka (Potato and Cabbage)

This vegetarian casserole has its origins in the original Moosewood Cookbook by Mollie Katzen. I have made it this way for years!

Helpful Hint: *Make it a meal with sausages and a good Russian rye bread.*

6 servings

4 medium potatoes, about 1½ pounds
2 teaspoons salt
1½ cups cottage cheese
½ cup plain yogurt
½ cup sour cream
2 tablespoons butter
1½ cups chopped onion
½ teaspoon ground caraway seed
½ teaspoon dried dill weed
½ medium head of green cabbage, shredded
2 tablespoons cider vinegar
Freshly ground pepper to taste
1 tablespoon sesame seeds
½ teaspoon paprika

Preheat the oven to 350°.

1. Cut the potatoes into 2" cubes. In a large pot, cover with water, add 1 teaspoon salt and boil until tender, about 15 minutes. Drain and return potatoes to the pot. Mash well and stir in cottage cheese, yogurt, and sour cream.

2. Melt the butter in a large frying pan. Add the onion and sauté until translucent, about 3 minutes.

3. Add the ground caraway, dill, cabbage, and the remaining 1 teaspoon of salt. Sauté until the cabbage is tender.

4. Combine the cabbage and onion with the mashed potato mixture. Stir in the vinegar and season with more salt and pepper to taste.

5. Spoon into a greased casserole dish. Sprinkle the top with the sesame seeds and the paprika. Bake, uncovered, 35 to 40 minutes.

Spicy Chinese Potatoes

East meets West!

Helpful Hint: *Use a large cast iron skillet if you have one.*

4 to 6 servings

3 or 4 medium white potatoes, very thinly sliced
The Sauce
    3 tablespoons soy sauce
    2 tablespoons rice vinegar
    1 teaspoon sugar
    ¼ teaspoon red pepper flakes
3 tablespoons vegetable oil
2 cloves garlic, minced
3 scallions, sliced in 1" pieces
1 serrano chili pepper, stemmed, seeded and sliced
Garnishes:
1 tablespoon toasted sesame seeds
Chopped fresh cilantro

1. Soak the potato slices in salted water for 5 minutes. Drain and pat dry.

2. Whisk together the soy sauce, rice vinegar, sugar, and pepper flakes with 1 tablespoon of water in a small bowl.

3. Heat the vegetable oil in a 10" cast iron skillet over high heat for a few minutes, until the oil is shimmering. Add the potatoes and fry, turning every minute or so, until the potatoes are fork-tender.

4. Add the garlic, scallions, and Serrano pepper to the pan. Continue to sauté for 1 minute, until the garlic is fragrant. Drain excess oil.

5. Pour in the prepared sauce from step 2 and toss well. Cook, turning frequently, for 1 to 2 minutes more.

6. Garnish with toasted sesame seeds and chopped cilantro to serve.

Australian Stuffed Spuds

Aussie style: Aussie Wendy is a friend of my sister, Mary. Wendy's family owned a restaurant in Australia called "Spud Mulligans." This popular potato presentation was called "Aussie Spuds." Over the top, but so what! So delicious!

4 servings

4 large baking potatoes (Wendy liked "Sebagos")
6 slices bacon, diced
½ cup chopped onion
4 large mushrooms, chopped
Garlic butter
½ cup grated cheddar cheese
Sour cream
Minced green onions or chives

1. Prepare baked potatoes, page 13.

2. While potatoes are baking, fry diced bacon in a frying pan. Remove to a paper towel-lined plate. Reserve 1 tablespoon of the drippings in the pan.

3. Fry the chopped onion and chopped mushrooms in the bacon drippings until the onion is translucent and the mushrooms are wilted.

4. Using tongs to hold the hot potatoes, cut a cross lengthwise and side to side on the top of each spud. Squeeze gently to open. Gently flatten the potato inside with a dinner knife.

5. Put a good dollop of garlic butter on the potato. Add diced bacon, fried onion and mushrooms, grated cheddar, and sour cream. Sprinkle with minced green onions or chives.

Note: *To make garlic butter, mash together ¼ cup softened butter with 1 to 3 minced cloves garlic. Add salt to taste.*

Wendy says:

Serve decorated with a tiny Australian flag! So there!

Peruvian Roasted Potatoes

Peru is the birthplace of the potato. The purple potatoes grown in Peru are a dry, starchy variety, which makes them good for roasting. Like other deeply colored fruits and vegetables, they are high in antioxidants. Heirloom purple potatoes are now widely available.

Helpful Hint: *You can use a mix of purple, red, blue and yellow potatoes. Choose small young potatoes, called "fingerlings," and cut large ones so they are a mostly uniform size.*

6 servings

Seasoning mix:
4 tablespoons olive oil
1 tablespoon Mexican oregano
1 tablespoon minced garlic
½ teaspoon salt
¼ teaspoon freshly ground black pepper
2 pounds purple potatoes (or a combination of colored potatoes)
Non-stick cooking spray
¼ cup snipped fresh cilantro

Preheat the oven to 400°.

1. Blend olive oil and seasonings together in a large bowl. Add the potatoes and toss to coat the potatoes evenly.

2. Choose a shallow roasting pan or casserole, large enough to hold all of the potatoes in one layer. Prepare the pan with non-stick cooking spray. Add the potatoes and spread evenly.

3. Roast for 35 to 45 minutes, stirring and tossing at least twice. The potatoes are done when they start to look shriveled and brown in spots.

4. Sprinkle with the cilantro to serve.

Nopalitos Con Papas (Cactus with Potatoes)

An authentic Mexican dish! Nopales are prickly pear cactus paddles. You can find them in Mexican markets, trimmed, with the small thorns removed and dark bumps peeled away. Diced nopales are called nopalitos.

Helpful Hint: *Use fresh nopalitos if you can find them. Frozen or canned will also work.*

4 to 6 servings

16 ounces nopalitos, cut in 1" dice
2 tablespoons vegetable oil
3 all-purpose potatoes, boiled and diced (about 1 pound)
1 small onion, diced
1 small tomato, diced
1 jalapeno pepper, diced small
1 teaspoon chili powder
Salt and black pepper, to taste

1. Boil the nopalitos in salted water for 5 to 8 minutes. Drain and rinse several times in a colander. (This will make them less gooey.)

2. Heat the vegetable oil in a large skillet. Add the cooked, diced potatoes and sauté until the potatoes just start to turn golden, about 3 minutes.

3. Add the onion to the skillet and sauté until the onion is translucent.

4. Stir in the nopalitos, tomato, jalapeno, chili powder, salt and pepper. Continue to stir and fry for several minutes, until everything is heated through.

Mexican Roasted Potatoes

Roasted potatoes with a bit more zip!

6 servings

Seasoning mix:
½ teaspoon ground cumin
½ teaspoon chili powder
½ teaspoon dried oregano
⅛ teaspoon garlic powder
⅛ teaspoon onion powder
Pinch ground cinnamon
½ teaspoon salt
¼ teaspoon freshly ground black pepper
3 large or 6 medium potatoes (about 2 pounds)
2 tablespoons olive oil
Non-stick cooking spray

Preheat the oven to 400°.

1. Blend seasonings together in a small bowl.

2. Cut each potato into 6 or 8 uniform wedges. Place in a large bowl and toss with the olive oil. Sprinkle with the seasoning mix and toss again to coat the potato wedges evenly.

3. Choose a shallow roasting pan or casserole, large enough to hold all of the potatoes in one layer. Prepare the pan with non-stick cooking spray. Add the potato wedges and spread evenly.

4. Roast for 45 minutes, stirring and tossing at least twice. The potatoes are done when they start to look shriveled and brown in spots.

Green Chile Stew

On one of our first visits to New Mexico, our friend, Ellie Sanchez, served us this stew. She called it "chile," and she served it over beans. It was nothing like the dish I knew as "chili," but it was delicious.

Helpful Hint: *The best chiles are from Hatch, New Mexico. If you can't find them, look for Anaheim chiles.*

Another Helpful Hint: *This recipe can be doubled easily.*

4 to 6 servings

2 tablespoons canola oil
½ pound beef round steak, cubed
½ pound lean pork cutlets, cubed
1 small onion, chopped
1 large clove garlic, minced
4 medium white potatoes, cubed
6 to 8 green chiles, roasted, peeled and chopped (see note)
1 teaspoon salt
½ teaspoon pepper
½ teaspoon cumin
½ teaspoon Mexican oregano

1. Heat the oil in a large pot until very hot. Add the beef, pork, and onions. Sauté until meat has browned and onions are translucent.

2. Add 4 cups of water and the cubed potatoes. Bring to a boil, cover loosely, and simmer until the potatoes and meat are tender, about 25 minutes.

3. Add the remaining ingredients. Cover loosely and simmer another 15 minutes.

4. Serve in bowls with warm tortillas or corn bread. Ladle the stew over some beans, as Ellie did, if you wish.

continued...

Note: To roast chiles, hold over a gas burner with tongs, turning to blacken all over. Alternately, roast on a gas or charcoal grill, searing on all sides for about 10 minutes. Place in a plastic bag or covered bowl until cool enough to handle. Strip off the peel and remove the stem and seeds. It's a good idea to wear plastic gloves when working with hot chiles to avoid getting the capsaicin (chile oils) on your hands. It doesn't wash off easily and may irritate your skin and eyes.

Another Note: If you absolutely are unable to locate fresh chiles, 6 ounces of frozen, roasted chiles will do. As a last resort you can use 1 or 2 (4-ounce) cans of roasted chiles.

Breakfast Burritos

In New Mexico, where I live now, potatoes are everywhere. This is a local favorite. Green Chile Sauce is useful in many dishes.

Helpful Hint: *There are many variations on this recipe. Try starting with Yellow Jacket Potatoes (page 138).*

4 to 6 servings

2 tablespoons butter
2 tablespoons canola oil
4 medium white potatoes, grated
1 small onion, chopped
Salt and pepper
8 slices bacon, cooked until crisp
4 to 6 eggs, fried, scrambled or poached
4 to 6 large flour tortillas, warmed
2 cups New Mexico green chile sauce, warmed (recipe below)
4 to 6 ounces mild cheddar cheese, shredded

First you have to make

New Mexico Green Chile Sauce

1 tablespoon canola oil
½ cup chopped onion
2 cloves garlic, minced
2 teaspoons flour
1 cup chopped roasted green (Anaheim) chile (substitute frozen chile or 2 [4-ounce] cans chopped green chile)
1 cup chicken broth

1. Heat the oil in a small skillet. Add the onion and garlic and sauté until the onion is transparent, about 2 minutes.

2. Sprinkle with the flour. Stir together over low heat for about 30 seconds.

continued...

3. Stir in the chopped green chile and the chicken broth. Bring to a boil and simmer gently until the sauce has blended and slightly thickened, about 3 minutes.

Now to the Burritos themselves...

Preheat the oven to 400°.

1. Heat the butter with the oil in a large frying pan until very hot but not smoking.

2. Add the grated potatoes, spreading to a depth of ¼".

3. Cook, covered, over medium heat until browned on the bottom.

4. Turn with a spatula and brown on the other side. Don't worry if you can't flip the potatoes all in one piece.

5. Add salt and pepper to taste.

6. Spoon a portion of the potatoes onto a warmed tortilla. Top with 1 or 2 slices of bacon and 1 egg (fried, scrambled or poached). Roll up into a loose cylinder and place seam-side down on a baking dish. Repeat with remaining tortillas.

7. Top the burritos with the chile sauce and sprinkle with the shredded cheese.

8. Bake until the cheese is melted, about 5 minutes. Serve hot.

Part 9: Make it a Meal

The First TV (at the farm), and Second TV (at home)

Salade Niçoise
Ham and Potato Scallop
End of the Trail Chili Dinner
Cottage Pie (or Shepherd's Pie)
Corned Beef Hash
Pinto Bean and Potato Chili
Salmon Salad with Potatoes and Berries
Yellow Jacket Potatoes

The Farm, from the air, circa 1955

The First TV (at the farm) and Second TV (at home)

Loring Air Force Base (AFB) was built in the mid-fifties, just ten miles from Fort Fairfield. The Air Force families were used to the amenities found in more up-to-date areas than Aroostook County. The new arrivals brought with them a taste for and an expectation of television. Those military folks missed their TV's! They launched the first TV station in The County (call letters: LAFB).

TV came first to Fort Fairfield households who were strategically close to the Strategic Air Command base, or in a strategic direction not interrupted by pesky hills and trees. Unfortunately that did not include our house, which was at the foot of a large hill that blocked the signal from LAFB TV.

At that time, about 1956, my grandmother was living with her sister, Louise, on the family farm, two miles from town.

The farm was up river to the west, and on the south bank, better suited to receive the TV signal from the base. The big box with the grainy black and white picture was an immediate hit. We pestered our parents constantly to visit Gram and Louise at the farm.

Shows were broadcast for only a few hours in the evening. Wednesday evening became our favorite for spending a couple of hours watching a local variety show (hosted by a Loring personality named Bill), followed by Red Skelton. Didn't we just love Clem Kadiddlehopper!

I think this was about the same time we discovered TV dinners. Everyone could choose his own favorite! Just pop those little aluminum trays in the oven. Want to know what the mashed potatoes tasted like? Did you ever try wallpaper paste? Were you expecting a recipe? Sorry!

After a few years of too much visiting at the farm, Dad decided there must be a way to get TV reception at our house. We just needed a TV antenna tall enough to catch signals over the top of the hill! No problem! The antenna that went up on the top of our roof was perched on a tower that rose about 100 feet into the sky. Now, you may think I am exaggerating, but I am not! My father wanted TV! The tower was stabilized by wires that attached to nearly every shingle on the roof. And, yes, it looked just as peculiar as you imagine.

This was a fine idea at first. With the antenna, the TV reception was no worse than most in our town. There was a box on top of the TV that

126

controlled the antenna's direction. We squabbled over it constantly, trying to improve the picture quality.

I was away at school when a lightning strike hit the antenna tower. I was not there to witness the event or the immediate destruction of the TV. The fire on the roof was put out quickly, and luckily the house did not burn down.

Within a year my father was part of a new venture called "Able Cable," which brought cable TV to The County. The picture quality was much better, and there were two more local stations originating from nearby Presque Isle. Shortly thereafter came Public Television, and my father fell in love with Julia Child. Now we are ready for a recipe!

**Dressed for Dinner at Loring AFB Officers' Club
Katherine, Mary, Charlie, Bobby**

Salade Niçoise (with Tuna and Green Beans)

The very best way to make this salad is with a fresh tuna steak that you have cooked yourself on the grill. This is still an excellent salad when made with your favorite canned tuna.

Helpful Hint: *Plan ahead to use leftover potato and green beans from the night before.*

4 servings

2 medium potatoes
½ pound fresh green beans
2 (6-ounce) cans tuna, drained (or 12 ounces fresh tuna, grilled)
¼ cup finely chopped celery
2 tablespoons minced onion
¼ cup finely chopped red or green bell pepper
¼ cup grated carrot
½ cup Dijon vinaigrette dressing (see recipe on the next page)
Garnishes:
    2 cups fresh greens
    1 tomato cut in wedges
    8 to 12 black Niçoise, Kalamata or Greek olives
    2 tablespoons shredded fresh basil and/or minced parsley

1. Microwave the whole potatoes until just soft. Microwave or steam the green beans until they are crisp-tender. Set aside to cool.

2. Mix together the drained tuna, celery, onion, bell pepper and grated carrot.

3. Cut the potatoes into small cubes. Cut the green beans in 1" pieces. Add the potato and green beans to the salad and toss with ¼ cup of the Dijon vinaigrette dressing. Continue adding dressing to taste.

4. Mound each serving on a bed of fresh greens. Decorate each serving with tomato wedges, olives, basil and/or parsley.

Dijon Vinaigrette

Yield: ¾ cup

¼ cup extra virgin olive oil
¼ cup canola oil
¼ cup wine vinegar (white or red)
1 tablespoon Dijon mustard
1 clove garlic, peeled
¼ teaspoon salt
⅛ teaspoon pepper
1 teaspoon sugar
Pinch of dried oregano and/or basil (optional)

Shake all ingredients together in a jar with a tight-fitting lid.

Note: *This dressing is delicious on your favorite tossed greens.*

Basil

Ham and Potato Scallop

A traditional dish, especially in the northern part of The County.

Helpful Hints: *You can use a thick slice of ham from the deli. Long, slow baking is the key to this scallop.*

8 to 10 servings

2 pounds russet potatoes (about 6), peeled and sliced in ⅛" slices
½ teaspoon salt
½ teaspoon freshly ground pepper
3 tablespoons flour
1 medium onion, thinly sliced, separated into rings
8 to 12 ounces ham steak, cut in small chunks
1 pint heavy cream (or part milk)

Preheat the oven to 300°.

1. Lightly butter a 13" x 9" x 2" glass baking dish.

2. Layer one-third of the potato slices in prepared baking dish, overlapping slightly. Sprinkle with salt, pepper and 1 tablespoon flour. Sprinkle half of the onion slices and half of the ham chunks over the potatoes. Repeat. Top with the remaining potato slices and sprinkle with the rest of the salt, pepper and flour.

3. Pour the cream evenly over the potatoes.

4. Cover the baking dish tightly with foil. Bake for 2 hours. Uncover after the first hour. Test by piercing the potatoes with a knife to see if they are tender.

5. Remove from the oven. Let stand 15 minutes before serving.

My friend, Jerry, suggests sprinkling ½ cup grated cheddar on top. Jerry is an excellent cook!

End of the Trail Chili Dinner

At the end of a two-week camping trip, six of us concocted this fabulous dish from our leftovers. (You can make this easily at home.) When camping, we rely on our friend, Jerry, who has an oven in his camper.

6 servings

1 tablespoon canola oil
½ medium onion, diced
1 large or 2 small zucchinis
1 clove garlic, smashed
½ teaspoon dried oregano
Salt and pepper to taste
4 potatoes, baked or cooked in a microwave, sliced in ½" slices
3 cups leftover or canned chili with beans
1 cup grated cheddar cheese
Garnishes
    minced scallions
    sour cream
    crushed tortilla chips

Preheat the oven to 350°.

1. Heat the oil in a medium skillet. Add the onion and cook over medium low heat for about 2 minutes. Add the zucchini and garlic and continue to cook and stir for 2 minutes more, until the vegetables are softened. Sprinkle with the oregano, salt and pepper.

2. Layer the potatoes, chili, and zucchini mixture in a large casserole or baking dish.

3. Cover the baking dish tightly with foil, and bake at 350° for 30 minutes, until heated through.

4. Remove foil and sprinkle with cheese. Return to the oven for 5 to 10 minutes, until cheese is melted.

5. Serve with optional garnishes.

Cottage Pie (or Shepherd's Pie)

A traditional dish, this is sometimes called "Shepherd's Pie" if it is made with ground lamb. This is one of my sister Mary's favorite recipes.

Helpful Hints: This is not as complicated as it looks!

5 to 6 servings

For the topping:
 4 to 5 potatoes (about 1½ pounds), peeled and quartered
 ⅓ cup cream
 ¼ teaspoon nutmeg
 ½ teaspoon salt
 ¼ teaspoon freshly ground pepper
 2 eggs
For the filling:
 1 tablespoon olive oil
 1 tablespoon butter
 1 cup chopped onions
 1 cup shredded carrot
 1 clove garlic, minced
 1½ pounds lean ground beef
 3 tablespoons flour
 ½ cup dry red wine
 1 cup tomato sauce
 1 teaspoon ground sage
 ½ teaspoon salt
 ¼ teaspoon freshly ground pepper
 1 (10-ounce) package frozen peas, slightly thawed

Start the topping first:

1. Boil the potatoes in salted water until tender, about 20 minutes. Drain and return to the pot.

2. Mash well, adding the cream, nutmeg, salt and pepper. Beat in the eggs, one at a time.

While the potatoes are cooking:

Preheat the oven to 375° after step 2.

3. Heat the olive oil and the butter in a large skillet. Sauté the onion, carrot and garlic until soft.

4. Crumble the ground beef into the skillet. Continue to cook and stir until the meat is nicely browned. Drain excess fat.

5. Sprinkle the meat mixture with the flour and stir well to mix. Add the wine and tomato sauce. Continue to cook and stir until the sauce is thickened.

6. Stir in the sage, salt, pepper, and slightly thawed peas.

Assemble the pie:

7. Turn the meat mixture into a greased 2½ -quart casserole or large (13" x 9") baking dish. Spread evenly over the bottom.

8. Spoon the potato topping over the filling, spreading evenly to the edges.

9. Bake at 375° for 45 minutes, or until the potatoes are puffed and golden.

Mary, in her favorite bathing suit

Corned Beef Hash

A good choice for brunch or supper.

Helpful Hint: *You can use a slice of corned beef from the deli, a can of corned beef, or leftover corned beef brisket.*

4 servings

1 pound (about 3) russet potatoes, diced
1 tablespoon olive oil
½ teaspoon dried thyme
½ teaspoon dried oregano
½ teaspoon dried basil
Salt and freshly ground pepper, to taste
2 tablespoons butter
2 cloves garlic, minced
1 small onion, diced
8 ounces corned beef, cut in small chunks
2 teaspoons Worcestershire sauce
Salt and freshly ground pepper
4 eggs, poached
Chopped fresh parsley (optional)

Preheat the oven to 400°.

1. Lightly oil a 13" x 9" x 2" baking dish with non-stick spray.

2. Place the diced potato in the prepared baking dish. Drizzle with the olive oil. Sprinkle the thyme, oregano, basil, salt and pepper. Toss to combine. Bake 18 to 20 minutes, tossing again after 10 minutes, until brown and crisp.

3. Melt the butter in a large skillet over medium heat. Add the garlic and onion. Cook, stirring, until the onions are translucent, about 3 to 4 minutes.

4. Stir in the corned beef chunks and cook, stirring, until lightly browned, about 3 minutes. Stir in potatoes and Worcestershire sauce. Cook, stirring, until heated through. Season with more salt and pepper, to taste.

5. Poach 1 egg per serving. Spoon the corned beef hash onto 4 plates. Make a well in the middle of each portion and add the poached egg. Garnish with parsley, if desired.

Pinto Bean and Potato Chili

A tasty vegetarian dish if you use vegetable broth.

Helpful Hint: *This chili doesn't mind being reheated.*

4 to 6 servings

1 tablespoon canola oil
1 medium onion, diced
2 poblano chiles, seeded and diced, or 1 (4-ounce) can diced chiles
1 clove garlic, minced
2 teaspoons ground cumin
1 teaspoon chili powder
Pinch of red pepper flakes
3 red or Yukon gold potatoes, cut in ½" dice. (about 12 ounces)
1 (15-ounce) can vegetable or chicken broth
1 (15-ounce) can diced tomatoes
2 (15-ounce) cans pinto beans, drained, rinsed, and lightly mashed
1 teaspoon salt
Optional garnishes:
    minced fresh cilantro
    sliced radishes
    sour cream
    grated mild cheddar cheese
    Bottled hot sauce, for serving

1. Heat the oil in a large pot with cover. Add the onion and cook over medium low heat for about 2 minutes. Add the poblano pepper (or diced chilis) and garlic and continue to cook and stir for 2 minutes more, until the vegetables are softened.

2. Add the chili powder, ground cumin and pepper flakes. Stir for a few seconds until the spices are fragrant.

3. Add the diced potatoes and broth. Add a little water, if needed, to just cover the potatoes. Bring to a boil. Lower the heat, cover, and simmer 10 to 12 minutes, until potatoes are tender.

4. Add the tomatoes (with their juice), beans, and salt, and mix well. Cover the pot and simmer the chili at the lowest possible heat for 15 minutes more, stirring occasionally. Add more water or broth if the consistency becomes too thick.

5. Serve with optional garnishes and hot sauce.

Salmon Salad with Potatoes and Berries

My favorite supper at The Range, a local restaurant.

2 servings

The Dressing:
    3 tablespoons canola oil
    1 tablespoon maple syrup
    1 tablespoon cider vinegar or raspberry vinegar
    ½ teaspoon salt
    Freshly ground pepper

The Salad:
    2 small red potatoes, boiled and cooled
    ½ pound salmon fillet, seasoned and grilled
    3 ounces mixed salad greens
    6 to 8 ripe strawberries, halved
    ½ cup blueberries
    ¼ cup pecans or candied pecans

1. Whisk all the dressing ingredients together in a small bowl.

2. Grill the salmon fillet until the thickest part flakes with a fork.

3. Toss the salad greens in a large bowl. Add dressing to taste. Toss again. Arrange on 2 large plates.

4. Cut potatoes into quarters, and nestle around the side of the greens. Add equal portions of the strawberries, blueberries and pecans. Top each serving with one-half of the grilled salmon.

Yellow Jacket Potatoes

This recipe was adapted from the Caribou Cook Book, printed in 1966. It has been a family favorite for over 50 years!

Helpful Hint: *Use leftover baked or boiled potatoes. Or cook them in the microwave before you plan to serve them.*

4 servings

8 slices bacon
1 small onion, roughly chopped (about ½ cup)
3 to 4 cooked potatoes, peeled and diced (about 3 cups)
Salt and freshly ground pepper
5 eggs
2 tablespoons milk

1. Fry bacon in a large skillet until crisp. Drain on paper towels, crumble and reserve.

2. Pour off and discard all but 2 tablespoons of the bacon fat in the skillet. Sauté the onion in the bacon fat until soft.

4. Add the potatoes and sprinkle generously with salt and pepper. Continue to sauté until the potatoes are heated through and browned in spots.

4. Beat together the eggs and milk. Pour over the potatoes and onion. Stir lightly with a fork and continue to cook and stir until the eggs are set.

5. Top each serving with the crisp bacon to serve.

Part 10: Other Good Stuff

Boston Marathon, 1988
New England Baked Beans
Cowboy Beans (Pork and Pinto Beans)
Killer Sweet Potatoes
WeaselSnot Memories and Recipes
Blueberry Muffins
Meadow Muffin Soda Bread
Recipes as Memories
Rita's Biscuits

Boston Marathon, 1988
Maggie and Me

Boston Marathon, 1988

Why on earth would anyone want to run a marathon? It was one of my mother's favorite questions. I can still hear her clucking as she pondered aloud what damages I was inflicting on my body.

In all, I have run ten marathons, all but one of them as a registered participant. So, officially, I have run nine. After my fourth marathon I "qualified" to register for the prestigious Boston Marathon. That meant that, at age 43, I had finished a certified marathon of 26.2 miles in less than 3 hours and 30 minutes.

The Boston Marathon is like the Kentucky Derby, the Indianapolis 500, and the Super Bowl. In other words, it is a big, show-stopping tradition that galvanizes spectators and participants. It is held on Patriots' Day, which is a Monday in April, and a legal holiday in Maine and Massachusetts. Paul Revere's Ride, remember? Maine was part of Massachusetts back then. And, no, the marathon route does not follow Paul Revere's route.

It was raining in Hopkinton that morning, and it looked like a long, chilly day ahead. My friend and I wondered why we were not smart enough to be in the business of manufacturing plastic trash bags, which were clearly the fashion statement of the day... the best way to stay dry and warm after you have parted with your sweats and your duffle bag! The first mile of the route was soon to be littered with discarded green trash bags.

The dreariness of the weather was no match for the adrenalin, energy and anticipation of the 12,000 runners. I was surprised to find that my number, W-147, seeded me quite far to the front. I would not have to wait very long after the starting gun.

I had several remarkable experiences during my first Boston Marathon. After the first few miles I found myself running with a pack of other runners who were all wearing matching orange t-shirts. As I looked closely I could see from their shirts that these people were an organized group of athletes from Oregon who all had developmental challenges. Every special athlete was accompanied by a personal helper, who assisted him or her along the course. I was in awe of the commitment and dedication of those runners and their helpers.

A bit later I looked up to see that the fellow running just ahead of me was wearing a shirt that said on the back, "Hi, I'm Sy. Say Hi as you go by." So

140

of course I did. Sy and I ran together for a couple of miles. He had lots of friends and fans along the course, and I began to be sorry that I wasn't wearing a shirt with my name on it! Later I read about Sy in Runners' World magazine. He was a well-known runner in the Boston community, a professor at MIT, and in his 80's at the time.

Soon after Sy and I parted, I glanced to my left to find that I was running next to a wheelchair. Not one of the wheelchair athletes, but a man being pushed in a wheelchair by another runner. Dick Hoyt and his son Rick, who had cerebral palsy, were competing as "Team Hoyt." I was starting to feel very emotional about all the incredible stories I was witnessing. I shared this with the runner on my right. When I glanced down I realized that he was running on a prosthetic leg, his right leg, from his knee to his sneaker. We were averaging about an 8-minute-per-mile pace at that time.

As we approached Wellesley we could hear first a rumble, then a roar. The Wellesley girls were out in force to cheer the runners on. I remembered a day in 1961 or 1962 when I was at Dana Hall in Wellesley. A group of us had walked down Grove Street to watch the runners go by and add to the cheering. I believe there were about 100 runners that day!

These wonderful, awe-inspiring experiences kept me going in the chilly rain until I got to Newton, where my daughter, Maggie, joined me for the last six miles. Maggie looked terrific! Fresh as a daisy and cute as a button! Not cold, not weary, not bedraggled. And, best of all, she was wearing a shirt that said "Maggie." My chosen shirt for the day said "Maine Track Club," so those hollering encouragement would shout, "Go, Maine!" which was not so bad, but sometimes, "Go, Track Club!" Ah, gee...... As the marathon route headed into the party belt of Boston College and Boston University, Maggie was everyone's favorite. I did my best to snatch some of the energy that was hurled at her. With every "Go, Maggie!" she would reply, "Go, Maggie's Mom!"

At the end of the race the participants were handed space blankets and Chunky Bars. Maggie thought that was a bit incongruous, as there were absolutely no chunky people around.

So why run a marathon? Aside from the personal glory, that is? My eyes still fill up with tears when I think back to the extraordinary things I witnessed that day, over 30 years ago.

In 2014, after the Boston Marathon bombing, I felt a kinship, a deep connection, with all of the other runners who had ever participated in that famous race. I think if you were to ask any of us, you would be told that we were all holding hands that day.

These things, not the personal thrill and feelings of accomplishment, are the reasons for running in the Boston Marathon.

Two Made-From-Scratch Baked Bean Recipes

Another important regional food question concerns the bean. What is the difference between "Boston Baked Beans" and "Maine Baked Beans?" All New England style beans involve long slow baking, with salt pork and molasses. In Mass the favorite bean is the Pea Bean, which is small and white. Mainers prefer Yellow Eye Beans, Jacobs Cattle Beans, or Soldier Beans. Pinto Beans are the favorite in the Southwest.

New England Baked Beans

My favorite beans are called "Soldier" beans. They are large white beans, about ¾" long, and if you turn them sideways you can see the little brown soldier in the center. Yellow Eye beans are similar, but a bit smaller than Soldier beans. Jacobs Cattle beans are larger, and spotted like a cow.

Helpful Hint: *Remember to sort, rinse, and begin soaking the dry beans the night before you plan to cook them. The cooking time is long, but the actual preparation is very easy.*

8 to 10 servings

3 cups dry beans
1 teaspoon baking soda
½ pound salt pork cut in 3 or 4 pieces
1 medium onion, sliced (about 1 cup)
½ cup brown sugar
⅓ cup molasses
1 teaspoon dry mustard
½ teaspoon salt
2 tablespoons cider vinegar

1. Pick over the beans and discard any that look rotted, and any pebbles that may have gotten into the bag. Rinse the beans and put them in a large cooking pot. Add the baking soda and enough water so the beans are covered by at least 3". (The baking soda will help to leach out the gas-producing sugars.) Set aside overnight, about 8 to 10 hours.

2. Drain the beans and return them to the pot. Add fresh water and bring to a boil over medium heat. Simmer gently for 1 minute. Drain again, skimming off any foam.

3. In a bean pot, or a slow cooker*, layer the beans with the salt pork and the onion slices.

4. Blend together the brown sugar, molasses, dry mustard and salt in a small bowl. Pour about 1 cup of boiling water into the bowl to help blend and dissolve the sugar. Pour this mixture over the beans in the bean pot.

5. Add more boiling water until it almost covers the beans.

6. Cover the pot and bake at 300° for 6 to 8 hours, until the beans are soft, but not mushy. Check the beans occasionally and add more boiling water as needed.

7. Add the cider vinegar during the last hour of cooking.

A slow cooker works well for cooking beans. It will not heat up your kitchen for a whole day! Try using the "high" setting. The liquid should be just barely simmering. Check often to see if the beans are cooked.

Soldiers or Soldats

Cowboy Beans (Pork and Pinto Beans)

Cowboy Beans make a great "stand-alone" casserole. Add some potato salad and cornbread to round out your meal. You can vary the amount of pork quite a bit, or leave it out entirely if you are serving other meat with your meal, or prefer a vegetarian dish.

Helpful Hint: *The cooking time is long, but the actual preparation is very easy.*

6 to 8 servings

3 cups dry pinto beans
1 teaspoon baking soda
1 tablespoon vegetable oil
1½ pounds pork cutlets, cut in 6 to 8 pieces
1 medium onion, sliced (about 1 cup)
1 green bell pepper, cut in strips
1 carrot, cut in small coins
3 cloves garlic, minced
2 tablespoons ground cumin
2 teaspoons chili powder
1 teaspoon oregano
1 (15-ounce) can diced tomatoes
1 teaspoon salt

1. Pick over the beans and discard any that look rotted, and any pebbles that may have gotten into the bag. Rinse the beans and put them in a large cooking pot. Add the baking soda and enough water so the beans are covered by at least 3". (The baking soda will help to leach out the gas-producing sugars.) Set aside overnight, 8 to 10 hours.

2. Drain the beans and return them to the pot. Add fresh water and bring to a boil over medium heat. Simmer gently for 1 minute. Drain again, skimming off any foam.

3. Heat the oil in a skillet and sauté the pork pieces until brown on all sides. Remove to a plate and set aside.

4. Add a little more oil to the skillet if necessary and sauté the onion, pepper, carrot and garlic until just barely wilted (about 3 minutes).

145

5. In a bean pot, or a slow cooker*, layer the beans with the pork and the sautéed vegetables.

6. Blend together the cumin, chili powder, oregano, diced tomatoes and salt in a medium bowl. Pour this mixture over the beans in the bean pot.

7. Add more boiling water until it almost covers the beans.

8. Cover the pot and bake at 300° for 6 to 8 hours, until the beans are soft, but not mushy. Check the beans occasionally and add more boiling water as needed. You should be able to see the water through the first layer of beans.

A slow cooker works well for cooking beans. It will not heat up your kitchen for a whole day! Try using the "high" setting. The liquid should be just barely simmering. Check often to see if the beans are cooked.

Killer Sweet Potatoes

This dish is a favorite for holidays and potluck gatherings. It never fails to bring raves and requests for the recipe!

Helpful Hints: *You can use a food processor, a hand mixer, or an old-fashioned potato masher to do the mashing. I prefer a masher. It is more of a workout, but there is less clean-up! Be sure to use real maple syrup and real vanilla.*

8 servings

Topping:
    ½ cup (packed) golden brown sugar
    ⅓ cup chopped pecans
    3 tablespoons cold butter
4 pounds sweet potatoes, peeled and cut in 1½" chunks
3 large eggs
2 tablespoons maple syrup
1 teaspoon vanilla extract
2 teaspoons fresh lemon juice
1 teaspoon salt

Preheat the oven to 350°.

1. Mix the brown sugar and pecans in a small bowl. Cut in the butter, using 2 knives or a pastry blender, until the butter pieces are the size of small peas. Chill in refrigerator until ready to use.

2. Cook sweet potatoes in a large pot of boiling water until soft, about 15 minutes. Test by piercing with a fork. Drain and return to the cooking pot. Mash well.

3. Beat the eggs, maple syrup, vanilla, lemon juice and salt in a medium bowl. Add to the sweet potatoes and mix well.

4. Butter a large (9" x 13") baking dish or 2½-quart casserole. Spoon in the sweet potato mixture. Sprinkle the topping evenly over the top.

5. Bake until the sweet potato mixture is set, about 1 hour.

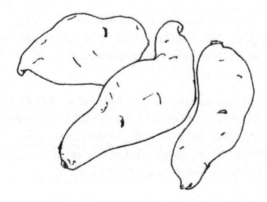

WeaselSnot Memories and Recipes

David and I moved into our house in Stockton Springs in 1988. It was a beautiful Cape Cod style house, which looked out, under a canopy of old maple trees, at Stockton Harbor. We didn't have to own, or pay taxes on, this lovely water view because we shared the front yard with the railroad tracks. The Bangor and Aroostook Railroad train lumbered by twice a day, carrying supplies, (mostly chemicals), for the paper-making industry. We found it quite tolerable, considering the benefits.

We thought our four combined children would fill up the upstairs bedrooms, but within a year the youngest had gone off to college, and all had summer jobs elsewhere. So we decided to turn the two upstairs bedrooms, with the nice views of the harbor, into a Bed and Breakfast. Playing up our close association with the railroad, we named it Whistlestop B&B.

The name "Whistlestop" actually had an earlier history on our property. A well-appointed touring railroad car that had belonged to the opera singer, Etelka Guerster, was bought by a vice-president of the Bangor & Aroostook Railroad, back in the early 1900's. He built a short spur off the tracks and backed the railroad car up onto what was later our front lawn. It was used as a summer cottage for fifty years, and was known to the locals as "Whistlestop." The railroad car cottage was dismantled and towed away in the 1950's when our house was built.

We made a sign for the end of the driveway, on which I painted a picture of the original Whistlestop railroad car. When our children came home from college for visits, they referred to our house as "Weasel Snot." It always helps to choose a good name!

We operated Whistlestop Bed and Breakfast for ten years. We were most busy during the summer tourist season, and we seemed to attract a lot of foreign travelers who preferred lodgings that were a bit off the road. Occasionally I served them potatoes for breakfast. The most requested breakfast item, however, was blueberry muffins.

148

Blueberry Muffins

Everybody's favorite muffin! When made with wild Maine blueberries, these can't be beat!

Helpful Hint: *Blueberries keep well in the freezer. Freeze them in a single layer on rimmed baking sheets. Once they are solidly frozen roll them into resealable plastic bags and store in the freezer.*

Helpful Hint #2*: Frozen blueberries have a tendency to become part of the batter. Put them in a small bowl with about a tablespoon of flour and roll them around a bit. They will keep their integrity that way and not turn your muffin batter blue!*

Yield: 12 muffins

½ cup butter, softened
¾ cup sugar
2 eggs
1 teaspoon vanilla
2 cups flour
1½ teaspoons baking powder
½ teaspoon baking soda
½ teaspoon salt
½ cup milk
1½ cups blueberries, fresh or frozen (lightly floured if frozen)
Cinnamon sugar for dusting

Preheat the oven to 375°.

1. Grease cups and tops of a 12-cup muffin tin.

2. Cream together the butter and sugar until fluffy. Beat in the eggs one at a time and stir in the vanilla.

3. Combine the dry ingredients (flour, baking powder, baking soda, and salt) in a separate bowl.

4. Add the dry ingredients to the egg mixture alternately with the milk and mix just until the dry ingredients are moistened. Gently fold in the blueberries.

5. Spoon the batter into the muffin cups, filling each half full. Sprinkle the tops lightly with cinnamon sugar, if desired.

6. Bake for 25 to 30 minutes. If using frozen berries, you may have to bake the muffins a few minutes longer. Cool before removing from muffin tin.

Meadow Muffin Soda Bread

You don't have to wait until Saint Patrick's Day to serve this Irish favorite! It looks like (ahem!) a meadow muffin, but it tastes delicious!

> 1 tablespoon corn meal
> Dry ingredients
>> 1¾ cups all-purpose flour, plus more for dusting
>> 1¾ cups whole wheat flour
>> 3 tablespoons toasted wheat germ
>> 3 tablespoons oat bran cereal
>> 2 tablespoons old-fashioned rolled oats
>> 2 tablespoons (packed) brown sugar
>> 1 teaspoon baking soda
>> ½ teaspoon salt
> 2 tablespoons chilled butter
> 2 cups (about) buttermilk

Preheat oven to 425°.

1. Grease a (12" x 16") baking sheet and sprinkle with the corn meal.

2. Combine the dry ingredients (all-purpose flour through salt) in a large bowl and mix well.

3. Cut butter into small pieces. Add to flour mixture and rub in with fingertips until mixture resembles fine meal and butter pieces are the size of corn flakes.

4. Stir in enough buttermilk to form a soft dough. Dust a smooth surface with flour. Turn out the dough onto the floured surface and knead a few times until the dough sticks together.

5. Cut the dough into 2 equal pieces and pat each piece into round shapes about 1½" high. Transfer to the prepared baking sheet.

6. Cut ½" deep slashes in the form of a cross on the top of each loaf.

7. Bake until bread is dark brown and a toothpick inserted in the center comes out clean, about 40 minutes. Cool completely on racks before serving.

Robert, in a Maine Potato Growers Hat

Recipes as Memories

Recipes are such wonderful ways to remember those loved ones who now are gone. I have many of my mother's recipes that I use on a regular basis, and quite a few from my Aunt Judy. There are even a few of my grandmother's recipes that make their way onto my table.

I get particular pleasure from recipes that have been passed along more than once, like Rita's recipe for biscuits. Each time I use one of these recipes I think of the person who wrote it, who made that dish, who bothered to cook it and share it with me. What a wonderful way to keep the memory of that person alive!

My mother's dear friend Rita passed away over twenty years ago. She was a Canadian, and she lived in the next town, just across the border. She and Mum played golf together regularly, traveled together, entertained together, shared many cups of strong King Cole tea, and more than a few cocktails. Rita had red hair and a personality to match. I can still hear Rita laughing, something she did most of the time.

A few years ago David and I bought a small cabin ("camp" to us Mainers) on a lake on the border, about 70 miles from where I grew up. Some neighbors who lived down the lake hailed us when we paddled by in our kayak. After a glass of wine we got to talking about food and recipes, naturally. My new neighbor, Barb, went inside her "camp" to fetch a recipe to show me. It brought tears to my eyes when I recognized Rita's handwriting on the old, tattered card. Barb and Rita had been friends many years before when they lived near each other as young women in Northern New Brunswick. When I realized that Barb had also known my mother, we both shed a few tears. Since then Barb and I have shared many fond stories, a few photographs, and, yes, more recipes!

Mum and Rita

Rita's Biscuits

My mother's friend, Rita, shared this recipe. Both Mum and Rita have been gone for many years, but I think of them both whenever I make these biscuits.

Helpful Hint: *A pastry blender works well for cutting the butter into the dry ingredients. If you don't have one you can use two knives, or cut the cold butter into small pieces and work it into the flour mixture with your fingertips.*

Yield: 18 to 20 medium biscuits

3 cups flour
1½ teaspoons baking soda
3 teaspoons cream of tartar
1 teaspoon baking powder
1 tablespoon sugar
8 tablespoons cold butter (1 stick)
1½ cups milk

Preheat the oven to 400°.

1. Sift together the flour, baking soda, cream of tartar, baking powder and sugar.

2. Cut the butter into the flour mixture until the butter pieces are the size of small peas.

3. Stir in about 1 cup of the milk. Continue to add milk until you have a soft, pliable dough.

4. Turn the dough out onto a lightly floured surface and knead lightly about 20 times. Pat out with a floured hand until the dough is about ½" thick.

5. Cut close together with a floured biscuit or cookie cutter. Fit leftover bits together without re-kneading to form more biscuits. Place on ungreased cookie sheet, close together if a soft side is desired, about 1" apart for biscuits with crusty sides.

6. Bake 12-15 minutes, until tops are golden. Serve warm.

Part 11: Sweets & Fun Things

The Old Box

Needhams (Potato Candy)
Potato Prints

The Almost Modern Age

Potato Play Dough
Taters for Tots

The Old Box

Several years ago David scanned every recipe in my old, tired and much-loved recipe file. He did it on the sly, and presented me with the disk as a birthday present. While I love having all those old recipes at my fingertips on the computer, and even stored in the "cloud" for easy access when traveling, I could not part with the old box. One of those old recipes, torn from a magazine, is called "The Bride Serves Duckling a L'Orange." My father's handwriting across the top suggests that I try it for Thanksgiving. I may never use the recipe again, but my father's handwriting is priceless. He died in 1968.

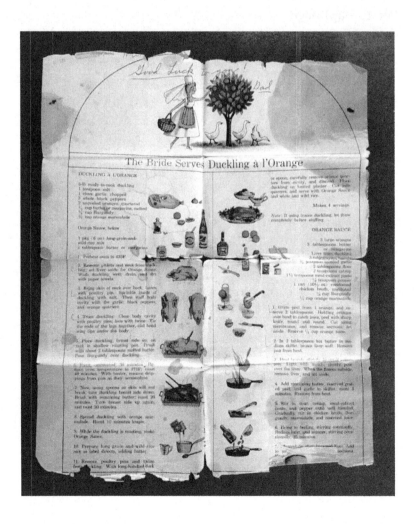

Needhams (Potato Candy)

Needhams are a traditional Maine potato candy. This recipe comes from an old cookbook called "Cooking Down East," by Marjorie Standish. I heard the candy was named for a traveling evangelist named Needham, who was much admired by a Maine candy maker.

Helpful Hint: *Do you "need 'em"? Well, maybe not, but I suggest you try some the next time you are in Maine!*

Many servings

The Center:
 2 medium potatoes, to make ¾ cup mashed potatoes
 ½ teaspoon salt
 ½ pound margarine
 2 pounds confectioners' sugar
 ½ pound flaked coconut
 2 teaspoons vanilla
The Coating:
 ½ cake paraffin (2½" x 2½")
 12 ounces semisweet chocolate chips
 4 (1-ounce) squares unsweetened chocolate

1. Peel the potatoes. Cut them in quarters and boil for 20 minutes, until soft.

2. Drain the potatoes and return them to the pot. Add salt and mash well.

3. Place the margarine in a double boiler and melt over boiling water. Add ¾ cup mashed potato, confectioners' sugar, coconut and vanilla.

4. Mix well and turn into a buttered jelly roll pan (10 ½" x 15 ½"). Spread evenly. Allow to cool until hardened. When hard, cut into 1" by 1½" pieces.

5. Using the double boiler again, melt the paraffin wax, then add the chocolate chips and unsweetened chocolate. Allow the chocolate to melt and stir well to mix the ingredients.

6. Dip the Needham pieces in the chocolate mixture, using a toothpick, a cake tester, or balanced on the tines of a fork. Allow excess chocolate to drip off before placing on waxed paper to harden.

Potato Prints

This technique is a wonderful way to create your own greeting cards, gift wrapping paper or t-shirt designs.

Helpful Hint: *Potato Prints are a fun project to do with kids. Little ones may need some help with the sharp knife.*

You will need:
Paper or fabric
Potatoes, any kind
Paring knives
Metal cookie cutters in various shapes
Paper towels
Paper plates
Kitchen sponge, paintbrush and/or small paint roller
Printers ink, stamp pad or fabric paint or printer's ink

1. Cut a potato in half. Press a cookie cutter at least ¼-inch into the cut surface of one half. Slicing across, cut away the potato around the cookie cutter using a paring knife, leaving the cookie cutter design. Remove the cut-away part of the potato. (You could also create your own design and cut around it with the paring knife.)

2. Dry the potato design with a paper towel so the ink or paint will adhere better.

3. Apply paint or ink to the potato design. If you are using printers' ink or fabric paint, pour a small amount on a kitchen sponge, and use that as you would a stamp pad. Alternately, pour some of the ink or paint onto a paper plate and use a paintbrush or small paint roller to apply the paint to your potato design.

4. Press the potato stamp down on the paper or fabric you wish to decorate. You may want to do a few practice stampings on scrap paper to get the hang of how much paint to apply and how hard to press.

More Helpful Hints: *Use a separate potato for each color, unless you want the colors to mix. Blot excess paint on a clean paper plate.*

The Almost Modern Age

When our children were young adults and just starting to have children of their own, they made it clear to us that now we were expected to travel to visit them for holidays, not the other way around. At one time it happened that two of the young families were living in New York and one young family was not too far away in Baltimore. The fourth was in Hong Kong, but being unencumbered by young children, they could travel great distances and leap tall buildings in a single bound, or maybe with one airline connection.

As the parents of this dispersed brood, we could travel by car from Maine, and still conjure up the Thanksgiving meal of their dreams. To be fair to the young mothers, their main concern was baby food and mothers' milk. The young fathers, on the other hand, needed turkey, maybe a little Wild Turkey, and mashed potatoes.

While I prefer to look the other way and hold my nose, when it comes to dried potatoes in a box, I must confess to using Betty Crocker's Mashed Potatoes with Sour Cream and Chives for that New York City Apartment Thanksgiving. And you know what? It wasn't half bad! All the sons-in-law praised my effort, and the resulting glue, as extremely tasty! So, if you have to go with the box, this would be my recommendation. I also recommend the Wild Turkey, without which the deception might not work!

In New York for Thanksgiving, 2000

Back: David, Peter, Rich, Dan, Joe, Rob
Front: Maggie (with Charlie), Dickey, Lucy (with Ian),
Katherine, Sin Wah, Anne (with Jesse in utero)

Potato Play Dough

Here is a fun activity to share with the little kiddoes... and possibly the best use for potato flakes!

Helpful Hint: *The dough is non-toxic, and edible, if not exactly tasty!*

You will need:

> Potatoes, any kind (alternately, instant potato flakes)
> Flour
> Salt
> Food coloring
> A work surface on which you can make a mess

1. Peel and cut up potatoes. Boil until soft; then drain well. Mash with a potato masher until uniformly mushy. Allow to cool.

2. Gradually add ¾ cup flour for each cup of mashed potato. Knead the whole mess with your hands. The more you knead, the more like play dough it will become. A little salt can make it easier to work with.

3. Work in a few drops of food coloring as you are kneading.

Alternately, and easier:

1. Mix together in a bowl, 2 parts instant potato flakes and 1 part flour. Add a bit of salt.

2. Add food coloring to water. Add the water to the potato flake and flour mixture a little bit at a time, until you have the right consistency. Knead, and play!

Taters for Tots

Try this!

You will need:

1 smallish baked potato per tot
Butter, salt and pepper to taste
Thin spaghetti, uncooked (not to be eaten)
1 carrot, scrubbed, cut in rounds for ears, cubes for noses
Peas or blueberries for eyes

A picture is worth a thousand words!

Index

Salads

Potato Salad,36
Mediterranean Potato Salad,38
German Sour Cream Potato Salad,39
Greek Potato Salad,40
Syrian Potato Salad,88
Hot Potato Salad,92
German Potato Salad,109
Salade Niçoise (Tuna and Green Beans),128

Soups and Stews

Clam Chowder,64
Corn Chowder,66
Fish Chowder,68
Cheesy Chowder,70
Vegetable Minestrone,71
Polly's Beef and Vegetable Soup,72
Vichyssoise,77
Patate Fricassee (Beef Stew with Spuds),83
Soupe aux Pois (Split Pea Soup),84
Green Chile Stew,121

Vegetables

Cabbage
Colcannon (Mashed with Kale or Cabbage),97
Russian Solyanka (Potato & Cabbage),113

Cauliflower
Cauliflower and Potato Gratin,54

Corn
Corn Chowder,66

Green Beans,
Potato and String Bean Salad,49
Salade Niçoise (with Tuna and Green Beans),128

Kale
Colcannon (Mashed with Kale or Cabbage),97

Onion
Onion Potatoes,56

Peas
Potato and Pea Salad,48
Soupe aux Pois (Split Pea Soup),84

Other Vegetables
Mashed Turnips & Potatoes,53
Cauliflower and Potato Gratin,54
Roasted Root Vegetables,57
Ratatouille,58
Polly's Beef and Vegetable Soup,72
Fiddleheads,93
Nopalitos Con Papas (Cactus with Potatoes),119
End of the Trail Chili Dinner,131
Killer Sweet Potatoes,146
Taters for Tots,163

Local Ethnic Favorites

Franco-American
Tourtiere (Pork Pie),80
Poutine (OMG Fries),82
Patate Fricassee (Beef Stew with Spuds),83
Soupe aux Pois (Split Pea Soup),84
Rappie Pie (Chicken and Grated Spuds),86

Lebanese or Syrian
Syrian Potato Salad,88
Swedish
Hasselback Potato Fans,89
Swedish New Potatoes,90
Hot Potato Salad,92
Native American
Fiddleheads,93

Alphabetic by Recipe Name

Made in the USA
Coppell, TX
04 December 2020

43071392R00098